آداب النكاح

The Proper Conduct of Marriage in islam

Adab An Nikah

Book Twelve of
Ihya' Uloom ud Din

Imam Ghazali

Translated By
Muhtar Holland

Qadeem Press

Qadeem Press Edition
Breathing Life into Forgotten Pages
www.qadeempress.com

Find our titles on your favourite online bookstore using the keyword 'Qadeem Press'

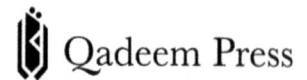

Contents

ACKNOWLEDGMENTS *vii*

TRANSLATOR'S INTRODUCTION *ix*

CONCERNING THE AUTHOR *xi*

Author's Introduction
Preamble to the book by the author,
Abū Ḥāmid Muḥammad al-Ghazālī 5

Chapter One
The Merits and Disadvantages of Marriage 7

Chapter Two
Circumstances of the Woman and Conditions of the Contract 43

Chapter Three
Conjugal Life.
Concerning the properties of conjugal life, and what takes place during marriage. Examination of the respective duties of husband and wife 59

ABOUT THE TRANSLATOR 97

Acknowledgments

All praise is due to Allāh, the Beneficent, the Merciful!

We bear witness that there is no god except Allāh, and that Muḥammad is the Messenger of Allāh!

Our Lord, thank You for giving us this wholesome task!

Translator's Introduction

Of all my translations, this one surely deserves the prize for patience, since it has waited twenty years for publication. (Patience is a virtue, of course, and perhaps especially in the context of marriage!)

In 1977, my rather large family and I spent several months at Wisma Subud, in Jakarta, Indonesia. I was about to take up a teaching post at the nearby International School, when, due to a dramatic shift in Indonesian government policy, it became impossible to obtain the necessary immigrant status. Our British passports assured us that Her Britannic Majesty would receive us with hospitality, so we flew in haste to London, via Singapore, Bombay and Moscow.

My dear brother and his wife performed the near-miracle of squeezing all nine of us into their tiny apartment. Then we found a home near Rochester, Kent, through the good offices of a somewhat unorthodox clergyman—who attached greater value to helping his fellow creatures than to observing formalities, whether ecclesiastical or governmental. The house had been condemned by the local council, on account of a road-scheme that had not been implemented. Though somewhat dilapidated, it was habitable enough, so I set to work in the basement—on my translation of Imām al-Ghazālī's "Proper Conduct of Marriage."

By 1978, when the translation was essentially completed, we had moved to Leicester, at the invitation of the Islamic Foundation. I declined an offer to publish the work in an edited form, because I felt that the reader deserved to know everything that Imām al-Ghazālī had to say. Several other translations of mine were published in the 1980's, following our move to the U.S.A., but "Marriage" failed to find a publishing mate. Then, in the early 1990's, the rights were acquired by Al-Baz, which is now poised to send the work to the printer. May the reader be as well pleased as the translator!

Muhtar Holland

February, 1998

Concerning the Author

Abū Ḥāmid Muḥammad ibn Muḥammad ibn Muḥammad ibn Aḥmad aṭ-Ṭūsī al-Ghazālī was born in A.H. 405/1058 C.E., and his earthly life ended in A.H. 505/1111 C.E. As the surname "aṭ-Ṭūsī" indicates, his birthplace was the Iranian town of Ṭūs.

For the Western reader, it may be helpful to note that al-Ghazālī was a small boy in 1066 C.E., the famous date of the Battle of Hastings. The Norman conquest of England would hardly have caused a stir in Ṭūs, but it did contribute to a shift in the balance of power between Christian Europe and the Islāmic world. It was during al-Ghazālī's lifetime that the First Crusade was launched, and Jerusalem was captured from the Muslims in 1099 C.E.

At the time of al-Ghazālī's birth, the Seljuq Turks had assumed a leading role in the Islāmic world. As well as defending Islām against the infidels from without, they were in conflict with powerful and dangerous schismatics, notably the Fāṭimid Shīʿa of Egypt. The Shīʿa saw in their leader something far more autocratic than a custodian of the Law who was himself governed by it. For them, the leader was himself the Law, since he was in receipt of infallible divine guidance. Their doctrines undermined the whole traditional basis of the main Islāmic community.

In response to the Fāṭimid challenge, the Seljuqs initiated an ambitious educational program. A vizier called Niẓām al-Mulk founded colleges in the major cities of the Seljuq domain, including Nishāpūr, where al-Ghazālī became a student. He proved a brilliant scholar in Islāmic jurisprudence *[fiqh]* and theology *[kalām]*, and was eventually appointed professor at the celebrated Niẓāmiyya University in Baghdād. As a powerful weapon in the ideological warfare with the Fāṭimids, he enjoyed favor in the highest circles.

The Crusaders and the Shīʿa were not the only enemies of traditional Islām. Another threat came from the philosophers, with their tendency to put human reason above the belief in divine revelation, on which the Islāmic community was founded. After making a profound study of philosophy, Imām al-Ghazālī delivered a fatal blow to its practitioners, in a work entitled *The Incoherence of the Philosophers*.

Despite his glittering success, Imām al-Ghazālī was inwardly dissatisfied, so he abandoned his career for the life of hardship, abstinence and devotion to worship. During ten years of wandering, he experienced a spiritual transformation, in which the Truth came to him at last, as something received rather than acquired. Blessed with an inner certainty, he then applied his outstanding faculties and vast learning to the task of revitalizing the whole Islāmic tradition. Through his direct personal contacts, and through his many writings, he showed how every element in that tradition could and should be turned to its true purpose. That purpose was to help the believer to live a life devoted to the service of Allāh, the One Almighty God, in constant remembrance of Him, and in preparation for the Life Hereafter.

Like most Muslims of his time, Imām al-Ghazālī wrote mainly in classical Arabic, though some of his books were written in the Persian language. His *magnum opus* is aptly entitled "The Revival of the Religious Sciences *[Iḥyā' 'Ulūm ad-Dīn]*." In its four volumes, the author deals with every aspect of the outer and inner life of the Muslim. The first volume covers the Islāmic forms of worship: ritual prayers, fasting, pilgrimage and so on. The second considers the behavior of the Muslim as member of a community of believers (including the Proper Conduct of Marriage). The third treats of the perils of the soul, and the fourth is devoted to the means of salvation. Largely because of this monumental work, he came to be known as *Ḥujjat al-Islām*, "the Proof of Islām."

May Allāh bestow His mercy upon him!

The Proper Conduct of Marriage in Islam

[Adāb an-Nikāh]

BOOK TWELVE OF IHYĀ' 'ULŪM AD-DĪN

بِسْمِ اللهِ الرَّحْمٰنِ الرَّحِيمِ

*Allāh bestows blessings
on whomever He will, without reckoning
(Qur'ān 24:38)*

INTRODUCTION

In the Name of Allāh,
All-Merciful and Compassionate.

Praise be to Allāh, Whose wondrous works are proof against the arrows of illusion, from Whose simplest marvels the minds of men reel, giddy and perplexed, and Whose tender blessings—be they chosen or unsought—abound for all creatures without cease.

His wonderful favors include His creation of man from seminal fluid (thereby giving rise to kinship and affinity) and His imbuing His creatures with a sexual appetite by which He coerces them to compulsive 'husbandry'[1] and maintains their progeniture by force and constraint.

Moreover, He has attached great weight to ties of kinship and values them highly; for their sake He has declared fornication unlawful, going to great lengths to make it repugnant by sanction and deterrent, and has made the committing thereof a heinous sin and an odious offense. He invites and urges us to marry, by commendation and by command.

Glory be to Him, Who decreed death for His servants and so abased them by wrecking[2] and shattering, then sowed sperm seeds in the ground of the womb, bringing forth new creatures to repair the destruction wrought by death: an intimation that the oceans of destiny flood the whole universe with benefit and detriment, good and evil, hardship and ease, winding and unwinding.[3]

[1] *ḥirātha*; an allusion to Qur'ān 2:223 ('Your wives are a tillage *[ḥarth]* for you [to cultivate]....').

[2] *hadm*; an allusion to the Prophetic Tradition (recorded by at-Tirmidhī): 'Remember often the wrecker of delights (*hādim / hādhim al-ladhdhāt*).' As Bauer points out, this last phrase became the standard epithet of Death in the stories of *A Thousand and One Nights*.

[3] *ṭayy wa-nashr*; the translation given above, with its suggestion of 'shrouding and unshrouding', represents an attempt to span the range between the literal meaning ('wrapping and unwrapping') and the figurative ('burial and resurrection').

Blessings upon Muḥammad, the Envoy sent with warning and good tidings, and upon his family and companions; blessings beyond count or reckoning, and many salutations.

Marriage comes to religion's aid, striking devils with dismay; it is a fortress firm against God's enemy, as well as a cause of the prolificity [of the Muslim community] in which the Chief of the Messengers will glory before the other Prophets [on Resurrection Day].[4] How appropriate that one should study its occasions, preserve its sacred traditions and its etiquette, explain its aims and purposes, and detail the paragraphs and chapters of the subject. Its most important precepts will be expounded in three chapters:

1. The pros and cons of marriage;

2. The proprieties to be observed in respect of the contract and the two contracting parties;

3. The right conduct of conjugal life from the time of the contract until separation occurs.

[4] The original sentence is in heavily rhymed and alliterative prose, impossible to reproduce in acceptable English. An effort to approximate might yield: 'Wedlock serves as duty's stay, leaving devils in dismay, against God's foe a fortress firm alway....'

CHAPTER ONE

Merits and disadvantages of Marriage

The scholars hold differing views on the virtue of marriage: at one extreme are those who insist that it is superior in merit to devoting oneself solely to the worship of Allāh; others, while acknowledging its merit, would give priority to divine worship, so long as the soul does not experience an unsettling craving for marital union and urge to coition; yet others hold it best to abstain in this day and age, although marriage had some virtue in former times, when there were legitimate ways of earning a living and when women's morals were not objectionable.

To discover the truth of the matter, we must first set forth the Prophetic and other traditions on either side of the argument, then proceed to discuss the advantages and the drawbacks of marriage. It should thus become clear whether marriage or abstinence commends itself to the individual, in the light of his immunity or vulnerability to those drawbacks.

The favorable view of marriage

a) Qur'ānic Verses:

Allāh (Exalted is He) has said:

> Marry the unwed among you.... (24.32)

This is a positive command. He also said:

> Do not prevent them from marrying their husbands. (2:232)

This put a stop to the practice of *ʿaḍl* (whereby a father could keep his daughter from getting married), and made it unlawful.

When praising and extolling His Messengers, the Exalted One said:

> And We sent Messengers before you, and We assigned to them wives and offspring. (13:38).

He mentioned that as a bestowal of grace and a mark of favor. Moreover, He has praised His saints for requesting it in their prayers of supplication, for He said:

> And those who say, "Our Lord, grant us through our wives and our offspring a cooling of the eyes [i.e., solace]...." (25:74)

It is said that only those Prophets who married are mentioned in the Qur'ān. Yaḥyā [John the Baptist] (may Allāh bless him and give him peace) did marry, they say, though without cohabiting (whether because his only desire was to acquire merit and to follow the noble precedent, or perhaps for modesty's sake). As for Jesus (peace be upon him), he will marry and have children when he descends again to the earth.

b) Prophetic Traditions *[akhbār]*:

The Prophet (Allāh bless him and give him peace) has said:

> Marriage is my exemplary way *[sunnatī]*; those who are averse to my example are also averse to me.[5]
>
> Marriage is my exemplary way; whoever loves my character *[fiṭratī]* should follow my example.
>
> Marry and multiply, then I shall glory in you before the nations on the Day of Resurrection: [in all of you,] even the miscarried fetus.
>
> He who dislikes my example is not of me; my example includes marriage, so let those who love me follow my example.
>
> He who abstains from marriage out of fear of impoverishment is not one of us.

(It is the pretext for abstention that is faulted here, rather than abstention *per se*.)

> He who has means should marry.
>
> He who can afford it should marry, for that is the best safeguard of modesty and chastity. Otherwise let him fast; the fasting will be a [form of] castration for him.

(This suggests that marriage is favored because of the danger of depravity in the eye or in the genitals. The word 'castration' *[wijā']*

[5] The context of this remark is included in the fuller versions recorded by al-Bukhārī and Muslim: A small group of Companions visited the homes of the blessed Prophet's wives, enquiring how he worshipped. In an excess of zeal, they declared their intention to pray without sleep, to practice unbroken fasting and to remain celibate. Urging moderation, Allāh's Messenger (Allāh bless him and give him peace) told them: 'I fast and I break fast, I pray and I sleep; I also marry women. Those who are averse to my example....'

signifies the contusion of the testicles of a stallion to take away its virility; here it is used metaphorically in the sense of 'sexual impotence induced by fasting.')

> If you find a newcomer commendably devout and trustworthy, then give him a woman in marriage; otherwise there will be discord and great corruption in the land.

(Here again the argument in favor of marriage is based on fear of corruption.)

> One who marries for the sake of Allāh, or gives in marriage for the sake of Allāh, earns the right to Allāh's friendship.
>
> He who marries secures one half of his religion, so let him beware of Allāh where the other half is concerned.

(This also shows that marriage is esteemed as a precaution against misconduct, providing security from corruption; for what most often corrupts a man's religion is his genitals and his belly, and by marrying he takes care of one of these at least.)

> The work of a human being is all cut short, but for three things: a righteous child who prays for him, alms he has dispensed, and religious knowledge he has imparted.

(The first of these is attainable only by way of marriage.)

c) Later Traditions *[āthār]*:

'Umar[6] (may Allāh be well pleased with him) said: "The sole obstacles to marriage are incapacity and immorality."

(Clearly implying that religion presents no obstacle to it, since he confines the obstruction to two blameworthy factors.)

Ibn 'Abbās[7] (may Allāh be well pleased with him and with his father) said: "The devotion of the devotee is not complete until he marries."

(Perhaps he would have it that marriage is both an act of devotion in itself and a means of perfecting one's devotion. More likely, however, we should take him to mean that only through marriage can one's inner feeling be relieved of the pressure of sexual passion, and that devotion

[6] 'Umar ibn al-Khaṭṭāb, a great Companion and the second Caliph *[khalīfa]* of the Prophet (Allāh bless him and give him peace).

[7] 'Abdu'llāh ibn 'Abbās (d. A.H. 68). A cousin of the Prophet (Allāh bless him and give him peace). He became a scholar of great renown, especially for exegesis of the Qur'ān.

remains incomplete unless the inner feeling[8] is undisturbed. For this reason, he used to summon his young protégés[9] when they reached puberty, telling them: "If you wish to marry I shall get you married, for if Allāh's servant commits a sexual offense he tears his faith from his heart.")

Ibn Mas'ūḍ[10] (may Allāh be well pleased with him) used to say: "If I had but ten days left to live, I would like to marry, so as not to meet Allāh as a celibate."

Mu'ādh ibn Jabal[11] (may Allāh be well pleased with him) lost two wives to the plague,[12] with which he was also stricken. "Find me a wife," he cried, "for I would not like to meet Allāh as a celibate."

(These last two sayings indicate that both men saw virtue in marriage for its own sake, not just as a precaution against the perils of passion.)

'Umar (may Allāh be well pleased with him) married frequently. He used to say: "I only wed for the sake of having children."

A certain Companion was totally dedicated to the service of Allāh's blessed Messenger, even sleeping at his house in case he needed anything during the night. "Won't you get married?" asked the Messenger (Allāh bless him and give him peace), but the man replied: "O Messenger of Allāh, I am a poor man with no possessions. Besides, I would have to give up serving you."

The question came up again later, to be met with the same response. Then the Companion pondered and said: "By Allāh, the blessed Messenger knows more of what is conducive to my welfare in this world and the Hereafter, and of what will bring me close to Allāh, so if he asks me a third time I will go and do it." When the question was indeed

[8] Lit. 'heart'. In Ṣūfī usage, however, *qalb* has a more comprehensive meaning. See: L. Zolondek, *Book XX of Al-Ghazālī's Iḥyā' 'Ulūm al-Dīn* (Leiden: E.J.Brill, 1963), pp. 3–4; also K, Nakamura, *Ghazali on Prayer* (Tokyo: The University of Tokyo Press, 1973), 51 nn.

[9] 'Ikrima and Kuraib among others. ('Ikrima [d. A.H. 105] became a famous Qur'ānic commentator.)

[10] Abū 'Abd ar-Raḥmān 'Abdu'llāh ibn Mas'ūd al-Hudhlī (d. A.H. 32 or 33). One of the earliest and closest Companions of the Prophet (may Allāh be well pleased with them all). A man of lowly antecedents, he became an authority on the recitation and interpretation of the Qur'ān, as well as an expert on Islāmic law and the Prophetic tradition.

[11] Abū 'Abd ar-Raḥmān Mu'ādh ibn Jabal ibn 'Amr ibn Aws al-Khazrajī (d. A.H. 17 or 18). One of the earliest believers, he became a learned and active Companion.

[12] The Plague of 'Amwās [Emmaus] claimed 25,000 victims in A.H. 17 or 18 (638/639 C.E.).

repeated, the man asked Allāh's Messenger to find him a wife. He was told to approach a certain tribe, saying: "Allāh's Messenger commands you to give me one of your young women in marriage."

Reminded of the man's absolute poverty, the Messenger told his Companions to collect for their brother a date-stone's weight of gold. They made the collection and escorted him to the tribe, whose people found him a spouse. The Prophet then ordered a marriage feast, whereupon some of the Companions got together to provide a sheep for the wedding banquet.[13]

(Such repeated urging suggests there is merit in marriage *per se*. It is of course possible that this particular individual displayed symptoms of needing to be married.)

A tale is told of how a devotee in one of the nations of yore surpassed in worship all the people of his epoch. The excellence of his worship was mentioned to the Prophet of his age, who said: "How good the man is, except for neglecting part of the exemplary way." The devotee was grieved to hear this and he asked the Prophet about it. "You omit to marry," he was told. "It is not that I hold it unlawful to do so," he replied, "but I am poor and dependent upon other people." The blessed Prophet then promised to give him his own daughter in marriage, and he was as good as his word.

Bishr ibn al-Ḥārith[14] said: "Aḥmad ibn Ḥanbal[15] is my superior on three counts: he pursues lawful gain for others as well as for himself, whereas I seek it for myself alone; he has an expansive approach to marriage, whereas my style is cramped; he has assumed the role of spiritual leader of the masses...."

It is said that Aḥmad (may Allāh have mercy on him, took a new wife on the second day after the death of the mother of his son ʿAbdu'llāh, saying: "I hate to spend one night in celibacy."

As for Bishr, when he heard that people were discussing his failure to marry and were calling him neglectful of the exemplary way, he said: "Tell them that he is preoccupied with absolute duty *[farḍ]* to the exclusion of what is but highly commended *[sunna]*." Rebuked on

[13] Part of the narration is actually in the first person, the speaker being the Companion in the story (Rabīʿa al-Aslamī).

[14] A Ṣūfī of the third Islāmic century (d. A.H. 277/841 C.E.).

[15] A prominent Traditionist and eponym of one of the four schools of Islāmic law (d. A.H. 241/855 C.E.).

another occasion, he said: "All that keeps me from marrying is the word of Allāh (Exalted is He): 'Women have rights equal to their duties, in fairness.'" (2:228). This was mentioned to Aḥmad, who exclaimed: "Bishr is incomparable! He keeps me in place like the point of a lance." Be that as it may, it is related that he appeared to someone in a dream and was asked: "How has Allāh treated you?" He replied: "I was accorded exalted rank in the Garden of Paradise, and allowed to look down upon the stations of the Prophets, yet I never attained the ranks of the married."

(According to another version of the story, his reply was: "Allāh said to me: 'I would have preferred you not to meet Me celibate.'") When asked what had become of Abū Naṣr at-Tammār, he said: "He was raised above me by seventy degrees." This evoked surprise: "How so? We should have thought you his superior." But he explained: "He earned that by his patience with his little daughters and his family burdens."

Sufyān ibn 'Uyaina[16] said: "Having many wives does not constitute this-wordliness. 'Alī (may Allāh be well pleased with him) was the most ascetic of the Companions of Allāh's blessed Messenger, yet he had four wives and seventeen concubines. Marriage is exemplary conduct from of old, and an innate disposition of the Prophets."

A man once said to Ibrāhīm ibn Ad'ham[17] (may Allāh have mercy on him): "How fortunate you are, to have dedicated yourself to worship through celibacy." But he rejoined: "Just one anxiety you suffer because of your family is worth far more than everything I am involved in." When the man asked him what then prevented him from marrying, he explained: "I feel no need of a wife, and I do not wish to be a disappointment to a woman."

It has been said that the merit of the married man exceeds that of the celibate as the merit of the holy warrior surpasses that of one who sits at home; also that one prayer-cycle performed by a married man is worth seventy performed by a bachelor.

[16] Abū Muḥammad Sufyān ibn 'Uyaina ibn Maimūn al-Hilālī (d. A.H. 196 or 198). A prominent scholar of Qur'ān and Tradition.

[17] Abū Isḥāq Ibrāhīm ibn Ad'ham ibn Manṣūr ibn Yazīd ibn Jābir at-Tamīmī al-'Ijlī (d. ca. A.H. 160). The Prince of Balkh who became an ascetic Ṣūfī. His life has often been compared to that of Buddha.

Traditions unfavorable to marriage

The Prophet (Allāh bless him and give him peace) has said:

> The best of men, two centuries hence, will be one who is lightly burdened, who has neither wife nor child.
>
> There will come a time for people when a man's downfall will be at the hands of his wife, his parents, and his children: they will reproach him with his poverty, and by demanding of him what is beyond his means they will get him into situations where his religion departs and he comes to perdition.
>
> A small family is one of the two forms of affluence, while a large family is one of the two types of poverty.

When asked about marriage, Abū Sulaimān ad-Dārānī[18] said: "Patiently doing without women is better than patiently enduring them, but to endure them is better than enduring the Fire."—"The single man experiences delight in work and tranquillity of heart unknown to the married man."—"I have never seen any of our com-panions marry and still maintain his original status."—"Three activ-ities betray an inclination toward this lower world: pursuing a career, marrying a wife, or transcribing traditions *[ḥadīth]*."[19]

Al-Ḥasan[20] (may Allāh have mercy on him) said: "When Allāh wishes a servant well He does not trouble him with family or wealth."

Ibn Abi'l-Ḥawārī[21] said: "Many have debated this saying, concluding eventually that it means not that one should do without these two things, but that one should possess them and not be obsessed with them." This echoes the words of Abū Sulaimān ad-Dārānī: "To be distracted from Allāh by family, property, or children—that is disastrous for you."

Summary

From no authority is disapproval of marriage reported in absolute fashion, without qualification. Arguments in favor of marriage, on the other hand, have come down to us both unconditional and qualified. It remains for us to unveil the subject by listing the drawbacks and the benefits of marriage.

[18] Abū Sulaimān ʿAbd.ar-Raḥmān ibn Aḥmad ibn ʿAṭiyya ad-Dārānī (d. A.H. 205 or 215). A Ṣūfī whose inclination lay toward extreme asceticism.

[19] Oral transmission was strongly preferred by most early authorities on Prophetic tradition, who sought to keep alive the spirit as well as the letter.

[20] Al-Ḥasan al-Baṣrī (d. A.H. 110). A religious leader of outstanding wisdom and piety.

[21] Aḥmad ibn Abi'l-Ḥawarī. A pupil of Abū Sulaimān ad-Dārānī.

The benefits of marriage

Marriage confers five benefits: a) children; b) the stilling of passion; c) good housekeeping; d) extended family ties; e) spiritual training through coping with all the foregoing.

a) The begetting of children

This is the essential basis upon which marriage was instituted, the purpose being continuance of procreation so that the world should never be devoid of human kind. Sexual desire was created only as a motivating incentive, entrusted as it were with the task of inducing the male to eject his seed and the female to accept insemination, gently luring the couple into 'catching' a child through their intercourse, rather like the gentle luring of birds into the net by scattering the grain they fancy.

Not that the Sempiternal Power would be incapable of creating individuals immediately, without recourse to insemination and mating, but the Divine Wisdom has ordained a sequence of effects from causes (though able to dispense therewith) to demonstrate His Power, to perfect the wonders of creation, to realize what was preformed by the Will, confirmed by the Word, and inscribed by the Pen.

The effort to beget children is a good work from four points of view, this being the main reason why marriage is encouraged even for those secure against the perils of passion (remember how none of the characters.we mentioned looked forward to meeting Allāh while celibate!)

Firstly, one conforms to the Will of Allāh by striving to produce offspring for the perpetuance of human kind. Secondly, one seeks to please Allāh's blessed Messenger by increasing the number of those who will be his source of pride. Thirdly, one looks for intercession through the supplication of the righteous child by whom one is outlived.

Fourthly, one looks for intercession through the little child who happens to die before oneself.

The first aspect is the most subtle, and the furthest removed from the comprehension of ordinary mortals, yet it is the most real and compelling to men of penetrating insight into the wondrous creation of Allāh (Exalted is He) and into the workings of His Wisdom.

By way of explanation, suppose a master gives his servant some seed and tools to farm with, provides him with a field ready for cultivation (of which the servant is capable) and appoints an agent to oversee his performance. Were this servant to prove lazy, damage the farming implements, leave the seed untended till it rotted, and use some trick to get rid of the agent, surely he would deserve the animosity and censure of his master.

Well, the Exalted One created the two spouses. He created the man's penis and testicles and the sperm in his spine, providing veins and ducts for it in the testicles. He created the woman's womb as an abode and receptacle for the sperm. Upon male and female alike He imposed the urgings of sexual appetite. These acts and these instruments bear eloquent testimony to their Creator's intention, and clearly proclaim their significance to all who possess a mind, apart from the fact that the Exalted Creator has made His intent explicit on the tongue of His blessed Messenger, in the words: "Marry, multiply!"

Since He has given an explicit command and has divulged the secret, it must follow that anyone who refuses to marry is shirking his farm work, wasting the seed, and leaving idle the appropriate tools created by Allāh; he sins against the purpose of creation and the Wisdom intelligible from the evidence of natural structure, which is written on these organs in a divine script unmarked with consonants and vowels, legible by everyone divinely endowed with insight to penetrate the subtleties of the Sempiternal Wisdom. For this reason the Sacred Law abhors infanticide and the practice of burying newborn girls alive,[22] because these prevent the fulfillment of being.[23]

Thus he who marries strives to fulfill the Will of Allāh (Exalted is He), while he who holds aloof is neglectful and wasteful of what Allāh

[22] This practice, called *wa'd*, was common in pre-Islāmic Arabia.

[23] The author notes: 'This is pointed to by those who say that coitus interruptus *['azl]* is one of the two species of *wa'd*.'

hates to see wasted. It was because the Exalted One wished mankind to survive that He ordered the feeding of the needy, stressing this and describing it as a 'loan,' for He has said:

> Who will lend Allāh an excellent loan? (2:245 and 57:11)

Here you might object: "To say that the preservation of posterity and life is dear to Allāh would suggest that extinction is hateful to Him, thereby drawing a distinction between death and life in relation to the Will of Allāh (Exalted is He). It is known, however, that both exist by virtue of His Will, and that Allāh is quite independent of the universe, so why should He prefer their living to their dying, their survival to their extinction?"

Understand, therefore, that what has just been stated is true, although the inference from it is false, for what we have said in no way negates the subordination of all beings, good and evil, useful and pernicious, to the Will of Allāh. Like and dislike are mutually contradictory, but as a pair they do not stand in contradiction to the Will. Much that is willed is disliked, and much that is willed is loved. Though acts of disobedience are disliked, they are nevertheless willed, while acts of obedience are not only willed but at the same time loved and pleasing. We do not say that unbelief and wickedness are pleasing and loved, but we do say that they are willed. Indeed, the Exalted One says:

> He is not pleased with unbelief in His servants. (39:7)

How then can extinction be on the same footing as survival in relation to approval or dislike on the part of Allāh (Exalted is He)? Indeed, He says:

> I never hesitate over anything as I hesitate to take away the soul of my Muslim servant. He is reluctant to die, and I hate to disappoint him, yet for him death is inevitable.[24]

These divine words, "for him death is inevitable," allude to the priority of the Will and to the predestination mentioned in the Qur'ān: "We have ordained death among you...," (56:60) and "Who created death and life." (67:2)

There is no contradiction between Allāh's saying: "We have ordained death among you...," and His words: "and I hate to disappoint him."

[24] A 'divine saying' *[ḥadīth qudsī]*, not part of the Qur'ān.

But to clarify the truth of this we are required to ascertain the meaning of the terms Will, like and dislike, and to explain their real significance.

The associations conjured up by these words relate in fact to the human will, to human likes and dislikes. How far from the truth, since the Attributes of Allāh (Exalted is He) are as remote from the attributes of His creatures as His mighty Essence is remote from their essence. Just as the essence of creatures consists of substance and accident, while Allāh's Essence is too sacred for that, and as that which is neither substance nor accident bears no relation to what is substance and accident, even so His Attributes bear no relation to the attributes of creatures.

These realities belong to the science of revelatory disclosure and behind them lies the mystery of predestination, which it is forbidden to disclose. Let us leave this topic and concentrate on the distinction we have observed between entering into marriage, on the one hand, and abstaining from it, on the other. He who follows the latter course extinguishes a line of descent which Allāh had continued down to him, generation upon generation, since Adam, on him be peace. Yes indeed, the man who refuses to marry has severed a chain of being, a previously unbroken chain linking his own existence to that of the blessed Adam. He dies truncated, without issue.

If the sole motive for marriage were to ward off lust, the plague-stricken Muʿādh would hardly have cried: "Find me a wife, lest I meet Allāh as a celibate!" You might perhaps object: "Surely Muʿādh had no expectation of children at that moment, so how do you explain his desire for marriage?" But to this I would reply as follows: The child is produced by sexual intercourse. Intercourse is brought about by the prompting of sexual appetite. which is an involuntary impulse. The only voluntary contribution a man can make is to procure the stimulus to sexual desire, and this can normally be anticipated. One who has contracted a marriage has therefore performed his duty and done what he had to do; the rest is beyond his own volition.

That is why marriage is recommended even for the impotent, for the stirrings of desire are hidden and not susceptible of observation. Indeed, the recommendation to marry extends even to the totally castrated person who can never expect children,[25] in much the same way as the bald man is recommended to pass the razor across his pate as others do (on Pilgrimage), following the example of the righteous ancestors. In the same vein, the practices known as *ramal*[26] and *iḍṭibāʿ*[27] are still recommended during the Pilgrimage. The original purpose of these was to demonstrate stamina in the face of the unbelievers, and the imitation of this display of fortitude became model conduct for later generations.

Such are the considerations informing their severe disapproval of abstinence from marriage, even in cases where sexual appetite is enfeebled.

The second aspect is the effort to please and satisfy Allāh's blessed Messenger by multiplying those who are to be his source of glory. (Allāh's Messenger, on him be peace, has referred to this point in explicit terms.)

Indicative of the importance of children from every point of view is the report that ʿUmar (may Allāh be well pleased with him) married often and that he used to say: "I only wed for the sake of having children." Then we have the traditions disparaging the barren woman, such as these sayings attributed to the Prophet (peace be upon him):

> To be sure, a mat in the corner of the house is better than a woman who does not give birth.
>
> The best of your wives is she who is very fertile and very affectionate.
>
> A swarthy woman who is prolific is better than a sterile beauty.

This shows that the quest for offspring goes further to advance the case in favor of marriage than does the quest for protection against the perils of lust, for a beautiful wife would be more effective in safeguarding her husband's chastity and modesty, and more likely to appease his desire.

The third point is that a man should leave behind him a virtuous child to pray for him, in accordance with the Prophetic tradition: "The work of a human being is all cut short, but for three things...."[28]

[25] The author adds this qualification: This recommendation is weak in comparison to that addressed to a man capable of insemination, the more so in view of its unfortunate corollary: it leaves the woman unfulfilled and is wasteful of her inasmuch as she fails to achieve her own purpose—a situation fraught with an element of danger.

[26] A quickened pace, between walking and running.

[27] Wearing the upper half of the Pilgrim garb in such a manner that the right shoulder is uncovered.

[28] See p. 9 above.

One of the three exceptions is the righteous child we have mentioned. According to another Prophetic tradition:

> Prayers are presented to the dead upon trays of light.

One might remark: "Maybe the child would not prove to be virtuous." This would be inapposite, however, for we are speaking of a believer and virtue is the norm with religious children, especially if one attends to their upbringing and directs them toward righteousness. Anyway, the believer's prayer for his parents is always beneficial, be he pious or profligate. A father is rewarded for his child's prayers and good deeds, for he has earned them; but he is not reproached with his bad deeds, since:

> One burdened soul does not bear the burden of another. (6:164)

Thus the Exalted One says:

> We shall join their offspring to them, and We shall subtract nothing from their work. (52:21)

(In other words: "We shall not subject them to any diminution of their deeds, and We shall add on their children as a supplement to their good works.")

In fourth place, consider the child who dies before his father, and so becomes an intercessor for him. These sayings are attributed to the Prophet (Allāh bless him and give him peace):

> The child pulls his parents along to the Garden of Paradise.
>
> He takes hold of his father's coat as I am now holding yours.
>
> The child is told to enter Paradise, but he pauses at the gate thereof in unremitting fury,[29] saying: "I shall not enter the Garden unless my parents are with me." So the order is given: "Admit his parents with him into the Garden."
>
> The infants will assemble at the site of the Resurrection, when all creatures are called to render their accounts. The Angels will be told to lead them off to Paradise, at the gate of which the little ones will pause. Here they will be greeted with: "Welcome to the offspring of the Muslims! Enter—no accounting is required of you." But they will ask: "Where are our fathers and mothers?"
>
> The warden will then say: "Your fathers and mothers are different from you. They have committed sins and evil deeds, for which they must account and face recompense." This will set the children hollering and banging in unison upon the gates of Paradise, whereupon the Exalted

[29] *muhbanti'an*; an uncommon word, explained as meaning 'filled with rage and anger.'

> Lord will say (although well Aware of them already): "What is this banging about?" The warden will explain: "Our Lord, it is the children of the Muslims; they refuse to enter the Garden without their parents." Then Allāh, (Exalted is He) will say: "Mingle with the crowd, take their parents by the hand and admit them to Paradise."
>
> He who loses two children is protected by a screen against the Fire.
>
> If someone loses three innocent children, Allāh admits him to Paradise through His superabundant mercy toward them.

(When someone asked: "Two likewise, O Messenger of Allāh?" he replied: "Two likewise.")

Once upon a time, a certain righteous man used to receive suggestions that he ought to marry, but it seemed he would always reject the idea. Then one fine day he awoke from sleep, crying: "Marry me! Marry me!" They found him a wife, then enquired what had come over him. The man explained: "Perhaps Allāh will grant me a child, then take him to Himself so that he becomes my forerunner to the Hereafter. I say this because of the vision I had in my sleep: It seemed the Resurrection was at hand. I saw myself amid the throng of creatures assembled at the site. I was parched with a terrible thirst, along with all the others in the throes of thirst and agony. As we waited in this sorry state, some babies suddenly appeared to mingle with the crowd; they wore kerchiefs of light and in their hands they carried ewers of silver and goblets of gold. To one after another they administered drink, making their way through the crowd and bypassing the majority. I stretched out my hand to one of them and said: 'Give me a drink, for thirst afflicts me,' but he replied: 'You have no child amongst us; we give drink only to our parents.' When I asked them who they were, they told me: 'We are Muslims who died in infancy.'"

According to one interpretation, the divine words,[30] "Go to your tillage as you will, and forward for yourselves," refer to sending children ahead of one to the Hereafter.

Conclusion

From these four points of view, it has become evident that the virtue of marriage resides primarily in its being a means of begetting children.

[30] Qur'ān 2:223.

b) Immunity from Satan; relief from craving; protection against the perils of lust

A pointer to this [second benefit of marriage] is the Prophetic tradition:

> He who marries secures one half of his religion, so let him beware of Allāh where the other half is concerned.

Likewise:

> Marry! Anyone who cannot do so should fast, because fasting will be a form of castration for him.

This consideration is hinted at in most of the traditions[31] we have cited, though it is subordinate to the first. Sexual appetite is an agent charged with procuring the begetting of children; marriage gives it a chance to do its job, pays its wages, and averts the evil consequences of its impetuosity. He who obeys his Master out of the desire to please Him is not the same as one who obeys merely in quest of deliverance from the perils of this agency.

Passion and procreation are both divinely ordained, and there is a link between the two. It would be wrong to say that the purpose is pleasure and that the child is a necessary by-product (as, for instance, relieving oneself is a necessary consequence of eating, but not an end in itself.) No, the begetting of children is the aim of nature and the divine Wisdom, while sexual appetite is merely an incentive thereto.

By my life, there is in sexual appetite yet another dispensation, apart from the impetus to procreation, namely the joy experienced in the sating of it. If only that delight were lasting, it would be unparalleled by any other joy. It gives a foretaste of the delights we are promised in Paradise, for the prospect of a bliss we had never tasted would fail to impress. The prospect of sexual intercourse would hardly stimulate the impotent, nor would the pleasures of kingship and dominion serve to excite the interest of the very young. One advantage of worldly pleasures is that the hope of enjoying them permanently in Paradise can act as a spur to the worship of Allāh.

Consider this Wisdom, this Mercy, this divine Providence! See how two lives derive benefit through this one appetite: an outer life and an inner life. The outer life is the life a man leads through the continuance

[31]Prophetic *[akhbār]* and non-Prophetic *[āthār]*.

of his line, which constitutes a kind of survival, while the inner life is the Otherworldly life. The bliss [of sexual satisfaction], deficient because it is so ephemeral, thus stimulates a desire for perfect bliss, for bliss everlasting, and serves as incentive to the worship which leads to its attainment. Desiring this so ardently, the creature finds it easier to persevere in the course that will bring him to such felicity in Paradise.

There is not one single atom of the human body, inside or out, nor indeed of the entire dominion of heaven and earth, that does not contain such subtleties and marvels of Wisdom as to baffle the mind. But these are revealed only to pure hearts, in the measure of their sincerity and to the extent that they shun the glamour, the charms and the perils of this lower world.

Inasmuch as marriage offers protection from the perils of lust, it is of religious importance for everyone who is not incapable through indigence or impotence, i.e., for the great majority of people. For rampant sexuality, unchecked by the force of the fear of Allāh, drags one into perpetrating foul abomination. To this the blessed Prophet referred when he cited the words of Allāh (Exalted is He): "otherwise there will be discord and great corruption in the land." (8:73)

If a man is restrained by the rein of the fear of Allāh, all that happens is that he prevents his organs from responding to lust, thus preserving his modesty and chastity. However, when it comes to guarding the heart against temptation and bad thoughts, this is beyond our freewill; indeed, the lower self never ceases to distract us with sexual concerns. Seldom does Satan give respite from his insinuations. He may tempt one even during the ritual prayer, going so far as to channel into the mind such sexual notions as, if uttered in his presence, would raise a blush on the coarsest man alive.

Allāh has full knowledge of man's heart, for the heart in relation to Allāh is like a tongue in relation to mortals. The principal concern of the seeker, aspiring to tread the path to the Other world, is his heart; but even persistent fasting does not put a stop to the problem of temptation, at any rate not for the majority of people, unless allied with physical weakness and indisposition. That is why Ibn ʿAbbās (may Allāh be well pleased with him) said: "The devotion of the devotee is incomplete until he marries."

This ordeal is universal; few indeed are spared it. According to Qatāda,[32] lust is what is hinted at in the Exalted One's words:

> Do not burden us beyond our strength to bear it. (2:286).

ʿIkrima and Mujāhid[33] are reported as saying that the words of Allāh, "and man was created weak" (4:32), mean that man cannot endure being without women.

Fayyāḍ ibn Najīḥ said: "When a man's penis erects, he can say farewell to two-thirds of his reason." (Someone else made a similar remark, preferring the expression "farewell to a third of his religion.")

Among the peculiar interpretations of the Qur'ān ascribed to Ibn ʿAbbās (may Allāh be well pleased with him) is the explanation that "The evil of the darkness when it lours" (113:3) refers to the erection of the penis.

This is an overwhelming affliction for you when it rears its head; neither reason nor religion can withstand it. Although it is fit to induce the two forms of life we spoke of earlier, nevertheless it constitutes Satan's most powerful weapon against mankind. The Prophet (Allāh bless him and give him peace) alluded to this when he said:

> I have never seen creatures deficient in reason and religion exert more power over intelligent men than you womenfolk!

That is entirely due to the arousal of desire.

In his prayer of supplication, the Prophet (Allāh bless him and give him peace) said:

> O Allāh, be my refuge from evil in my hearing, in my sight, in my heart, and in my sperm!

He also pleaded:

> I beg You to cleanse my heart and guard my genitals!

Can it be right for the rest of us to treat lightly something from which Allāh's blessed Messenger seeks divine refuge?

A certain virtuous man used to marry frequently, so that he seldom had fewer than two or three wives. When reproached by some Ṣūfīs, he asked: "Does any of you know what it is like to have passion agitate his heart, while he is sitting or standing before Allāh and attempting to

[32] Abu'l-Khaṭṭāb Qatāda ibn Diʿāma ibn Qatāda as-Sadūsī (d. A.H. 118). Learned in Qur'ānic exegesis and Islāmic jurisprudence, he was also an authority on Arabic poetry.

[33] Abū'l-Ḥajjāj Mujāhid ibn Jabr al-Makkī (d. A.H. 104). A disciple of Ibn ʿAbbās. A leading representative of the rationalistic tendency in Qur'ānic exegesis and Islāmic jurisprudence.

relate to Him?" When they admitted that they were often troubled by that kind of thing, he went on to say: "Had I been able to accept a condition like yours just once in my entire life, then I should not have married. As it is, whenever some inclination threatens to distract me from my state of devotion, I satisfy it, relax, and get back to my preoccupations. In forty years no sin has troubled my heart."

When someone criticized the Ṣūfī lifestyle, a religious man asked him: "With what do you reproach them?" When the critic accused them of eating too much, the man replied: "If you were as hungry as they are, you would eat like them yourself." To the charge that they also married too often, he replied: "If you were as modest and chaste as they are, you too would marry as they do."

Al-Junaid[34] used to say: "I need sexual intercourse just as I need food." The wife is in fact nourishment and a means of keeping the heart pure. That is why Allāh's Messenger (Allāh bless him and give him peace) commanded anyone who caught sight of a woman, and desired her, to couple with his wife, since that would dispel the temptation from his soul.

Jābir[35] (may Allāh be well pleased with him) reports that the Prophet (Allāh bless him and give him peace) once set eyes on a woman. He went to attend to his need with [his wife] Zainab, saying afterwards: "When a woman approaches, she does so as if she were a devil, so if any of you sees a woman and she takes his fancy, let him go to his wife, for with her it is the same as it would be with the other."

The Prophet (Allāh bless him and give him peace) also said:

> Do not visit women whose husbands are away, for each of you has Satan in his bloodstream.

When asked if this was true even of himself, he said:

> I am no exception, though Allāh has helped me against him, and so I am safe.

(Sufyān ibn ʿUyaina points out that the [unvowelled] Arabic word must be *aslamu* ['I am safe']; the reading *aslama* would mean that Satan had 'submitted' or 'become a Muslim').

[34] Abu'l-Qāsim al-Junaid (d. A.H. 298). A prominent Ṣufī, regarded as a leading exponent of the moderate or 'sober' approach to mysticism.

[35] Abū ʿAbdi'llāh Jābir ibn ʿAbdi'llāh al-Anṣārī (d. A.H. 68 or 73 or 78). A Companion who transmitted many Prophetic traditions.

It is likewise related of Ibn 'Umar[36] (may Allāh be well pleased with him), who was one of the more ascetic and scholarly Companions, that he used to break his fast[37] with sexual intercourse before eating. He would sometimes copulate before bathing and performing the sunset prayer. All this he did so as to leave his heart clear to worship Allāh, and to dispose of Satan's power to distract him. It is also related that he used to mate with three of his concubines before the late evening prayer during the month of Ramaḍān.

[Referring to the Prophet (Allāh bless him and give him peace),] Ibn 'Abbās said: "The best of this Community is he who has the most wives."

Since sexuality is very pronounced in the make-up of the Arabs, the devout among them were all the more disposed to do a lot of marrying.

For the sake of inner tranquillity, it is permissible to avert the danger of fornication by marrying a slave-girl—despite the consequence that any offspring will carry slave status, which is a kind of perdition. Because of this [unfortunate consequence], such marriage is forbidden to anyone who can afford to marry a free woman.

Nevertheless, slavery for the children is less grave than the ruination of faith. The child suffers only temporary annoyance in this life, whereas the abominable sin of fornication causes loss of the Life Hereafter, beside one single day whereof the longest earthly lives pale into insignificance.

It is related that one day, after the people had left a gathering at Ibn 'Abbās's place, a young man stayed behind. "Is there anything you need?" asked Ibn 'Abbās. "Yes," said the young man, "I wanted to ask you a question, but I was ashamed to do so in front of the people, and now I am afraid and in awe of you." Ibn 'Abbās then said: "A scholar stands *in loco parentis*, so tell me whatever you would tell your own father."

The youth explained: "I am a young man without a wife. Fearing that I might otherwise commit fornication, I sometimes masturbate. Is that a sin?" Ibn 'Abbās turned away from him, then said: "Ugh! Marriage

36 'Abdu'llāh ibn 'Umar ibn al-Khaṭṭāb (d. A.H. 73 or 74). Son of the venerable Caliph 'Umar and a revered Companion in his own right.

37 Fasting in the month of Ramaḍān is one of the fundamental religious duties in Islām. It is observed by abstaining during the daylight hours from food, drink, and sexual relations.

to a slave-girl would be better than that, although it is preferable to fornication or adultery."[38]

This indicates that the lustful bachelor is tossed about among three evils: the least of them is marriage to a slave-girl (despite the ensuing slave status of the offspring); masturbation is worse, but the most heinous of all is adultery or fornication.

Ibn ʿAbbās did not declare any of these things lawful in the absolute sense. The two lesser evils are both to be avoided if possible; they may only be resorted to as a precaution against falling into an even more serious offense, just as one may resort to eating carrion to avoid starving to death. But to prefer the lesser of the two evils is not to signify that it is absolutely lawful, nor that it is absolutely good. The amputation of a gangrenous hand is not a good thing in itself, though it is permitted as a means of saving someone from the jaws of death.

From this point of view, therefore, marriage does carry an advantage: not for everybody, but certainly for the majority. The sexual appetite is enfeebled in many people, due to senility, sickness or suchlike, so that this incentive to marry no longer applies to them, leaving only the matter of progeny mentioned earlier. This applies universally, with the solitary and rare exception of the person who has suffered total castration.

When a man's nature is so dominated by sexual desire that one wife alone would not suffice to keep him chaste, it is recommended that he take more than one (up to a maximum of four). All is then well, provided he enjoys the love and mercy of Allāh and feels inwardly content with these wives. Otherwise, substitution is recommended.

After the death of Fāṭima[39] (peace be upon her), her husband ʿAlī (may Allāh be well pleased with him) remarried in seven days.

Al-Ḥasan ibn ʿAlī has been called a 'super-marrier' *[minkāḥ]*; he married over two hundred women. He sometimes contracted four marriages at the same time, and sometimes divorced all four wives at once, taking others in their stead.

The Prophet (Allāh bless him and give him peace) once said to al-Ḥasan: "You resemble me both physiologically and psychologically

[38] The Arabic term *zinā* covers both adultery and fornication. A more accurate translation would be 'unlawful sexual intercourse', but this would assume a knowledge of Islāmic Law. For a technical definition, see J. Schacht, *An Introduction to Islāmic Law* (Oxford University Press, 1979), p. 178.

[39] The Lady Fāṭima, daughter of the blessed Prophet, became the wife of the latter's cousin ʿAlī ibn Abī Ṭālib and bore him two sons, al-Ḥasan and al-Ḥusain. May Allāh be well pleased with them all.

[khalqī wa-khulqī]."[40] He also said: "Ḥasan is from me and Ḥusain is from ʿAlī." (They say that his frequent marrying is one respect in which he takes after Allāh's blessed Messenger.)

Al-Muhgīra ibn Shuʿba[41] married eighty women. Some of the Companions had three or four wives, while those who had two were too numerous to count.

Once the cause is known, treatment must be suited to the sickness. Here the object is to quieten the soul, and this should be kept in view when deciding how many or how few to marry.

c) Relaxation and recreation for the soul

This [third benefit of marriage] is obtained by enjoying the company and sight of one's wife, and by shared amusement, whereby the heart is refreshed and strengthened in worship; for the lower self *[nafs]* is prone to boredom and inclined to shun duty as something unnatural to it. If constrained to persevere in something repugnant, it jibs and backs away, whereas if revived occasionally by pleasures it acquires new strength and vigor. In familiarity with women one finds the relaxation to banish care and to refresh the heart.

The souls of the pious need legitimate recreation, which is why the Exalted One said:

> That he may rest with her. (7:189)

ʿAlī (may Allāh be well pleased with him) said: "Refresh your hearts awhile; too much strain will make them dull."

The Prophet (Allāh bless him and give him peace) said:

> The intelligent man must observe three moments: a moment for conversing with his Lord, a moment for accounting with himself, and a moment devoted to eating and drinking; this last will help him with the other two.
>
> The intelligent man goes out after three things only: provisions for his journey back to the Other World, the improvement of his livelihood, or a pleasure that is not unlawful.

[40] According to Bukhārī and Muslim, these words were addressed to Jaʿfar ibn Abī Ṭālib (a cousin of the blessed Prophet), but other authentic traditions stress the unique resemblance between al-Ḥasan and his blessed grandfather.

[41] Al-Mughīra ibn Shuʿba (d. A.H. 49). His proverbial ingenuity earned him the nickname Mughīrat ar-Raʾy. At tl e time of his death he held the important post of Governor of Kūfa.

> Every active man has dynamic energy, and all dynamism must have an intermission. When someone's intermission is modelled on my example, then he is on the right path.[42]

Abu'd-Dardā'[43] used to say: "I distract myself with some amusement to give myself renewed strength for my subsequent duty."

This saying has been attributed to Allāh's blessed Messenger:

> I complained to Gabriel, on him be peace, of being too weak to copulate, and he recommended *harīsa* [an aphrodisiac paste of crushed spices and pepper, etc.][44]

If this is authentic, the object must have been to facilitate recreation. The purpose could not be to banish desire, since that would be excited by an aphrodisiac. Besides, to lose one's desire is to lose the greater part of this intimate enjoyment.

The Prophet (Allāh bless him and give him peace) said:

> I have been enamored of three things in this world of yours: perfumes, women, and my solace in ritual prayer.

This [relaxation] is therefore a further benefit, as no one will deny who has experienced spiritual weariness from meditations, exercises of remembrance and other kinds of work. This benefit is distinct from the previous two, extending as it does even to those who have suffered total castration and those who lack sexual desire.

There would surely be virtue in marrying with the intention of enjoying this particular advantage, though few regard this as the main purpose of marriage. The object is usually to have children, to ward off lust, or something similar. Besides, there are many people who find entertainment in the spectacle of running water, greenery and the like, and who do not need to chat and have fun with women in order to relax. It is all a matter of different conditions and different personalities, and these must be taken into consideration.

[42] The author adds this note of explanation: 'Dynamism *[shirra]*' is eagerness and endurance plus intensity and power, as displayed at the start of the novitiate. 'Intermission *[fatra]*' is pause for relaxation.)

[43] Abu'd-Dardā' al-Khazrajī al-Anṣārī (d. A.H. 32). A Companion renowned for his piety and devotion, as well as for his profound knowledge of the Qur'ān.

[44] As the author himself suggests, the authenticity of this tradition is doubted by most authorities.

d) Freedom from concern with running the household (and all the chores of cooking, making beds, cleaning dishes and preparing meals)

A bachelor would still have a hard time living at home by himself, even if he had no sexual desire to contend with. Constantly preoccupied with domestic chores, he would never have a moment to spare for study and work. A virtuous wife and good housekeeper is therefore an aid to religion, since these affairs must run smoothly if one is not to suffer distracting disturbances and vexations in daily life.

That is why Abū Sulaimān ad-Dārānī (may Allāh have mercy on him) said: "A virtuous wife is not of this world, because she frees you for the Hereafter." She gives you this freedom both by managing the household and by satisfying your sexual appetite.

Commenting on the Exalted One's words, "Our Lord, give us in this world something good" (2:201), Muḥammad ibn Ka'b al-Qurṭubī[45] said: "That means a virtuous wife."

The Prophet (Allāh bless him and give him peace) said:

> Let each of you have a grateful heart, a tongue that remembers, and a believing and virtuous wife to help him prepare for his Other Life.

(Notice how he links her together with remembrance and gratitude.)

In some commentaries, the Exalted One's words, "We shall make him live a good life" (16:97), are taken to refer to the virtuous wife.

'Umar ibn al-Khaṭṭāb (may Allāh be well pleased with him) used to say: "After belief in Allāh, a man can have no better gift than a virtuous wife. Some women are booty unparalleled; some are shackles from which there is no ransom." (By 'unparalleled' he means 'irreplaceable.')

The Prophet (Allāh bless him and give him peace) said:

> I have the better of Adam in two respects: His wife was his accomplice in rebellion, while my wives are my aids in obedience; his demon was an infidel, while my demon is a Muslim who orders nothing but good.

(He evidently counted their help in obedience as something meritorious.)

In this [fourth advantage] pious men may therefore seek an extra benefit, though it only applies to certain individuals who have neither steward nor housekeeper. Moreover, this benefit may be enjoyed without taking an additional wife; indeed, a combination is likely to disturb the peace and disrupt the household.

[45] A *Tābi'ī* (member of the generation after the Companions).

This benefit includes the purpose of increasing one's effective strength through the wife's family and the support of family ties. That is something one needs in order to repel evil and find security. Thus it is said: "Scorned is he who has no helper." The man who can find someone to protect him from evil is in safe condition and his heart is free to worship. Humiliation is disturbing to the heart, but strength in numbers drives humiliation away.

e) Self-discipline and training through custodianship and guardianship

Upholding the rights of wives, enduring their tempers, bearing the pain they cause, endeavoring to reform them and guide them on the path of religion, striving to make legitimate earning on their behalf, and seeing to the children's education—all of these are tremendously meritorious acts, for they constitute custodianship and guardianship.

Wives and children are a flock, and the merit of their custody is enormous. No one would shirk it except from fear of being unable to live up to its demands. Did not the blessed Prophet say:

> One day as a just caretaker is worth more than seventy years of worship. Is not every one of you a shepherd, and every one of you responsible for his flock?

Someone who works for the betterment of others as well as himself is not the same as one who works solely for his own benefit, and one who bears trouble with patience is not like one who enjoys comfort and ease. Enduring a wife and children is equivalent to fighting in Allāh's cause.

That is why Bishr said: "Aḥmad ibn Ḥanbal has the better of me in three respects: Firstly, in that he seeks legitimate livelihood for others as well as for himself...."

The Prophet (Allāh bless him and give him peace) said:

> What a man spends on his family is a form of alms, and a man will be rewarded for the morsel he raises to his wife's lips.

Somebody once said to a learned man: "Of every good work Allāh has given me a share," then he went on to mention the Pilgrimage, Holy War and so on. "How far you remain from the work of the saints *[abdāl]*," said the scholar. "And what is that?" asked the man. "Legitimate earning and supporting a family."

Ibn al-Mubārak[46] asked his brothers, with whom he was on campaign: "Do you know of any deed more meritorious than what we are engaged in?"

[46] Abū ʿAbd ar-Raḥmān ʿAbdu'llāh ibn Mubārak ibn Wāḍiḥ al-Ḥanzalī al-Marwazī (d. A.H. 181). An ascetic who studied under the great jurist Mālik.

They told him they knew of none, but he said that he did. When they asked him what it was, he said: "A decent man with a family gets up in the night and sees his little children lying uncovered, so he wraps them up and tucks them in with his own clothing. His deed is more meritorious than what we are engaged in."

The Prophet (Allāh bless him and give him peace) said:

> Anyone who prays well, has a big family and little money, and does not slander the Muslims, will be with me in Paradise like these two [fingers of mine].
>
> Surely Allāh loves the decent pauper, father of a family.
>
> If a man's sins are many, Allāh afflicts him with the care of a family, so that he may expiate them.

One of the early believers said: "Some sins can be expiated only through family worries," while Allāh's Messenger (Allāh bless him and give him peace) said:

> Some sins can be expiated only through the cares of seeking a livelihood.

He also said:

> A man who has three daughters, and who maintains them and treats them well until Allāh makes them independent of him, to him Allāh will grant Paradise irrevocably—irrevocably, unless he does something unforgivable.

(When Ibn ʿAbbās narrated this, he used to say: "By Allāh, that is one of the most extraordinary and exquisite Prophetic traditions!")

It is related that a certain devoutly pious man looked after his wife very well until she died, whereupon it was suggested to him that he ought to remarry. He refused, saying: "Loneliness will be more restful on my heart and more conducive to my endeavor," but he said later: "A week after her death I had a dream in which the gates of heaven seemed to have opened; it appeared to me as if men were descending, traveling through the air in succession, and as each came down he looked at me and said to the next behind him: 'This is the wretch!' The next agreed, as did the third and then the fourth. I was too scared to ask them about it until the last of them, a young man, passed me by. I said to him: 'You there, who is this wretch you are referring to?' — 'You,' he replied. — 'Why is that?' I asked. — "We used to exalt your deeds among those of the warriors in Allāh's cause, but a week ago we were ordered to leave your deeds with those who lagged behind. We do not know what offense you have committed.'" He then said to his brethren: "Find me a wife! Find me a wife!" From that time on he was never without a couple of wives, or three.

Among the stories of the Prophets (peace be upon them) we learn that the Prophet Jonah *[Yūnus]* (peace be upon him) once entertained a party of visitors. As he went in and out of his house, his wife annoyed him and henpecked him, but he said nothing. They were amazed at this, but he said: "Don't be surprised. I put this request to Allāh (Exalted is He): 'Whatever You are going to punish me with in the Hereafter, give it to me in advance in this world.' He said: 'Your punishment is so-and-so's daughter—marry her!' So I married her, and you see what I am putting up with from her."

Patient endurance of such things serves to train the soul, to subdue one's irascibility, and to improve one's character. When a man lives on his own, or sharing the company of people of good character, the secret vices of his soul are not brought to the surface, nor are his inner faults revealed. One who treads the path of the Other Life is therefore obliged to test his soul by exposing it to these kinds of instigation, and making it accustomed to bearing them patiently, so that his character becomes balanced, his soul disciplined, and his inner being purified of blameworthy qualities.

Supporting a wife is not only a training and a discipline, but also a providing and a caring and a form of worship in its own right. This, then, is one of the advantages of marriage, though it is of benefit to only two sorts of men:

First there is the man intent on effort, discipline and character training, because he is at the start of his journey. He may well see this as a method of striving and a means of self-discipline.

Then there is the sort of worshipper who is inwardly immobile and inactive in mind and heart, his works being those of the physical body—in ritual prayer, pilgrimage and so on. For him to work for his wife and children, through legitimate earning and attending to their upbringing, is more meritorious than acts of worship which involve only his body and do not contribute to the welfare of others.

A man of well-trained character, however, be it innate or the result of his previous efforts, and who is inwardly active and intellectually alert to knowledge both exoteric and esoteric—such a man ought not to marry with this aim in view. He has had sufficient training, while learning is more meritorious than worship through the labor of keeping a family. Learning is also a religious work, as well as more beneficial, more general, and more comprehensively useful to others than meeting the upkeep of a family.

Such then are the advantages of marriage in religion, on the strength of which it is judged to be a virtue.

The disadvantages of marriage.

The drawbacks of marriage are three:

1. The difficulty of obtaining a lawful income

This is the most serious drawback, namely the near impossibility of making a legitimate livelihood—something not all can achieve, especially in these times of unsettled living conditions. Marriage may cause one to make moral compromises in the quest for income, and to resort to unlawful means of meeting one's obligations, to the ruination of oneself and one's family. The bachelor is safe from this, but the married man usually gets into bad ways, following the whims of his wife and swapping the Other Life for the life of this world.

According to a Prophetic tradition, a man with mountain-like merits will be made to stand by the Balance; he will then be questioned about his custodianship of his family and how he looked after them, and about his wealth: how he came by it and how he spent it. In settling these demands he will use up all his accumulated good deeds, every last one. The Angels will proclaim: "This is the one whose merits were all consumed by his family on earth, and today he is in pawn for his deeds."

It is said that the first to fasten on to a man a the Resurrection will be his wife and his children. They will make him stand before Allāh (Exalted is He), saying: "Our Lord, give us our due from him! He left us in ignorance, feeding us unlawfully without our knowledge." Then Allāh will exact retaliation for them from him.

One of the early believers said: "When Allāh wishes a man ill, He empowers fangs (meaning a family) to savage him."

The Prophet (Allāh bless him and give him peace) has said:

> No one meets Allāh with a sin greater than that of having left his family in ignorance.

This drawback is widespread. Few can escape it without having inherited or legitimately acquired wealth sufficient to support a man and his family, as well as the ability to be satisfied and not want more. One so situated can indeed escape this predicament, as can a man whose skill enables him to earn a livelihood by legitimate means (such as woodcutting, hunting, or any craft independent of the authorities), and who is able to have dealings with good people of obvious integrity and of mainly legitimate means.

When Ibn Sālim[47] (may Allāh have mercy on him) was asked about marriage, he said: "It is the best course these days for a man assailed by overwhelming lust; like the ass which, having spied the she-ass, cannot be beaten off and loses all self-control. For anyone possessing self-control, however, it is better to abstain from marriage."

2. The difficulty of treating a wife properly

[The second drawback lies in] the difficulty of giving wives their due, of putting up with their character, and of bearing the trouble they cause. In general, this is less serious than the first drawback; it is easier to cope with, since the task of treating women properly and satisfying their needs is less onerous than the quest for legitimate income. However, there is also an element of danger here, since the husband is "a shepherd, responsible for his flock."

The Prophet (peace be upon him) has said:

> It is sin enough for a man to neglect those in his care.

It is also related that one who runs away from his family is like a runaway slave, a fugitive *[ābiq]*; neither prayer nor fasting is accepted of him till he goes back home. But he who fails to give women their due, even though he stays at home, is the equivalent of a runaway.

The Exalted One says:

> Guard yourselves and your families against a Fire.... (66:6).

He commands us to protect them from Fire, just as we protect ourselves. But a man may sometimes be incapable of fulfilling even his obligation to himself; if he marries, his obligations multiply and another soul is added to his own.

> The self incites to evil. (12:53).

[47] Ibn Sālim al-Baṣrī. A disciple of the Ṣūfī scholar Sahl at-Tustarī (d. A.H. 283).

The more souls there are, the more this incitement is likely to increase. That is why someone gave this excuse for not marrying: "My own soul is a trial to me, so how could I add another to it?" As the saying goes: "The mousehole is cramped as it is, yet the creature ties the broom to its tail."

Ibrāhīm ibn Ad'ham (may Allāh have mercy on him) made his excuses in similar vein: "I would not have a woman disappointed in me, and I have no need of them (meaning: of having to give them their due, protect them and satisfy them); it's all too much for me."

Bishr made the same kind of apology, saying: "What stops me getting married is the word of Allāh (Exalted is He): 'They have rights, just as they have duties' (2:228)." He used to say: "If I had to look after a hen I would be afraid of becoming an executioner on the bridge."

Sufyān ibn 'Uyaina (may Allāh have mercy on him) was once seen at the Sultan's gate. People said to him: "This is no place for you," but he replied: "Have you ever seen the head of a family affluent?" Sufyān used to say:

The bachelor's life is for me!
Though draughty the house, he has his own key,
And of bawling and shouting it's free.

This drawback is also widespread, if not to the same extent as the first. It affects everyone except the wise man of intelligence and good character, perceptive in the ways of women, patient with their tongues, resistent to their passions, keen to accord them their due, turning a blind eye to their faults, cleverly managing their nature. The common condition of man, however, is foolishness, coarseness, impetuosity, frivolity, bad character, and unfairness combined with the expectation of perfect fairness from others. In this respect, such people will undoubtedly degenerate still further in marriage. For them it is safer to remain single.

3. Worldly distractions

This [third drawback] is less important than the first and second. It lies in the possibility that a wife and children may distract a man from Allāh (Exalted is He). They may attract him to worldly pursuits, to providing a good life for his offspring by amassing and storing up great wealth for them, and to boasting of them and taking pride in their numbers.

Now, anything that distracts a man from Allāh—be it wife, wealth or children—is a misfortune for the person concerned. I am not suggesting that it invites unlawful conduct (that aspect has been dealt with under drawbacks one and two), but that it may lead to indulgence in lawful pleasures, to total absorption in dalliance and familiarity with women, and to an addiction to the enjoyment of them. Marriage is the source of a host of such distractions, which engross the heart night and day till a man has no time for reflecting on the Hereafter and making himself ready for it. That is why Ibrāhīm ibn Ad'ham (may Allāh have mercy on him) said: "He who marries gravitates toward this world." (That is to say, it tends to make one gravitate in that direction.)

Conclusions

All the drawbacks and advantages have now been listed. To pass absolute judgment in an individual case, in favor of marriage or of celibacy, would represent a failure to comprehend these various factors. These several benefits and disadvantages should rather be taken as a criterion and touchstone, which the aspirant can apply to himself. Suppose the drawbacks do not apply to him, while the benefits abound; he possesses legitimate means and a good character, is so completely earnest about his religion that marriage could not distract him from Allāh, and at the same time he is a young man who needs to calm his desire, living alone and needing a housekeeper and the support of a family group. For him marriage is indisputably the better course, quite apart from the opportunity it provides for trying to beget offspring. But when the advantages do not apply, while the drawbacks are combined, then celibacy is preferable.

If (as most often happens) the pros and cons are evenly matched, it then becomes necessary to strike an exact balance between the contribution the benefits will make to augmenting the man's faith, and what the drawbacks will contribute to its diminution. If there is a convincing preponderance on one side of the scale, the decision will be made accordingly. The most obvious advantages are progeny and the stilling of desire, while the most obvious drawbacks are the need to make a living by illegitimate means, and distraction from Allāh. Supposing these factors are in opposition, our advice would be as follows:

a) When a man is not in distress on account of desire, and the advantage of his getting married would lie in the attempt to produce offspring, whereas the drawback would be the need for unlawful earnings and distraction from Allāh—for him celibacy is better.

There is no good in anything that distracts from Allāh, and no good in unlawful earnings, nor is this double deficiency compensated for by the matter of children. To marry for the sake of having children is to strive in pursuit of a hypothetical child's life, whereas the spiritual detriment here is a hard fact. To preserve the life of one's own soul and to guard it from perdition is thus more important than the effort to produce offspring. The latter is profit, but spiritual welfare is capital. In corruption of religion lies the blotting out of the Other Life, and the loss of the capital. The advantage cannot therefore compensate for either one of these drawbacks.

b) In the case where, in addition to the matter of children, there is a need to do something about desire (because the soul is longing for sexual intercourse), the following distinctions must be made:

1. If the reins of piety are not strong enough to restrain a man, and he fears involvement in unlawful intercourse, it is better for him to marry. His options are to commit fornication or to live by illegitimate means, and to have an unlawful income is the lesser of the two evils.

2. If he is confident that he will not commit fornication, yet cannot keep his eyes off what is forbidden, abstaining from marriage is better. The forbidden gaze is unlawful, as improper earning is unlawful, but the earning is a continuous process and involves both the man and his family, whereas the forbidden gaze is an occasional thing, involving no one else, and of short duration. It is true that the forbidden gaze constitutes 'fornication of the eye,' but if the genitals do not follow suit, it is more readily pardonable that the consumption of illicit income. If, however, it is feared that the gaze may lead to the sexual offense, the case must be treated as one where there is a danger of fornication.

3. That settled, we come to the third case. Here we have a man strong enough to observe modesty of gaze, but not strong enough to repel thoughts distracting to the heart. For him too, it is better to abstain from marriage, in that the deed in the heart is more readily pardonable. It is only for acts of worship that the heart must be undisturbed, but one cannot worship properly at all if one consumes illicit earnings and feeds one's family from them.

This is how one should weigh up these drawbacks and benefits, and reach a decision accordingly. No one who has grasped this will experience any problems with our reports of how the early believers sometimes encouraged and sometimes discouraged marriage, since that is all a question of what is right in given circumstances.

You might ask me: "If a man is proof against all the drawbacks, which is better for him then: dedication to the service of Allāh, or marriage?" My answer would be: Let him combine the two, for marriage in its contractual aspect is not obstacle to such dedication; it is only the necessity of earning a livelihood that may pose problems. But if a man is capable of making a legitimate income, marriage is again to be preferred. The night and the spare hours of the day he can devote to the service of Allāh, and in any case it is impossible to persist in religious exercises without ever taking a rest.

Let us suppose, however, that a man is so constantly engaged in earning his livelihood that he has no free time for anything but the prescribed prayers, sleeping, eating, and using the toilet:

a) If this man is one of those who tread the path of the Hereafter only by way of supererogatory prayer, pilgrimage, and other such physical acts, then for him marriage is better, because legitimate earning and the support of his family, the begetting of children, and patience with the female character, all constitute forms of worship no less worthy than supererogatory devotions.

b) If, on the contrary, his way of worship is through knowledge, contemplation, and inner experience, and if earning a living would interfere with this, then abstaining from marriage is preferable in his case.

You might ask: "Why did Jesus (peace be upon him) abstain from marriage with all its benefits? And if dedication to the service of Allāh is the most meritorious course, why did our Messenger (Allāh bless him and give him peace) take so many wives?"

I would reply by saying that combining the two is the best course for one who is capable of it, who has the necessary stamina, and whose aspirations are so lofty that no preoccupation could distract him from Allāh. Our Messenger (peace be upon him) did possess this strength; he was capable of combining with marriage the merits of a life dedicated to Allāh. Notwithstanding his nine wives, therefore, he was wholly devoted to Allāh. For him, the satisfaction of sexual desire was no impediment, just as people engrossed in the management of worldly affairs are not hampered in their business by having to attend to their natural wants; they may appear to be attending to these needs, yet their hearts are absorbed in their ambitions and never forgetful of their concerns.

Allāh's Messenger (Allāh bless him and give him peace) was ranked so high that nothing in this world could bar his heart from the presence of Allāh (Exalted is Hẹ). Revelation came down to him when he was in his wife's bed.[48] When was such rank bestowed upon any other? It is hardly surprising that what disturbs mere rivulets makes no impression on the ocean! It is not proper, therefore, to measure others by his scale.

As for Jesus (Allāh bless him and give him peace), he certainly possessed a firm resolve, but he lacked the stamina and so chose abstinence. Perhaps his condition was such that he would have been adversely affected by preoccupation with a family, or unable to make a legitimate livelihood, or incapable of combining marriage with total dedication to worship. The Prophets know best the secrets of their own state, their contemporary situation regarding honest livelihood, the female character, the perils besetting a husband in marriage, and the attendant benefits. Whatever circumstances prevail, such that either marriage or abstinence happens to be preferable, it is our duty in every case to put the best construction on the actions of the Prophets.

Allāh knows best of all.

[48] The wife was 'Ā'isha (may Allāh be well pleased with her).

CHAPTER TWO

Concerning the Marriage Contract[49]

The Contract

The basic elements and conditions essential to valid and lawful marriage are four in number:

1. The consent of the marriage guardian *[walī]* or, in his absence, the sovereign *[sulṭān]*.

2. The agreement of the woman (if she is a non-virgin *[thayyib]* and has reached puberty; or if she is a virgin who has reached puberty, but is given in marriage by someone other than her father or paternal grandfather.)

3. The presence of two witnesses of manifest rectitude. (Even if they are unknown quantities *[mastūrān]*, we still judge the contract to be concluded, on the grounds of necessity.

4. An offer and immediate acceptance *[ījāb wa-qabūl]*, expressed in terms of 'marriage' or 'wedding' (or words of the same import, whether in Arabic or any other tongue), by two persons of full legal competence, neither of them being a woman. (These persons may be the husband and the marriage guardian, or their authorized representatives.)

The following practices are customary, though not essential:

i) A proposal of marriage *[khiṭba]*, offered in the presence of the guardian. (If the woman is a widow or divorcee, the proposal should await the expiry of her period of withdrawal *[ʿidda]*. No proposal should be made while that of another man is still being considered, because 'proposal over proposal' was forbidden [by the Prophet (Allāh bless him and give him peace)].

[49] In the present work, al-Ghazālī is not primarily concerned with the strictly legal aspects of marriage, which he therefore mentions only in summary form (and confining himself to the doctrines of the Shāfiʿī school of Islāmic jurisprudence.)

ii) A religious address *[khuṭba]* before the marriage. The praise of Allāh may also be mingled with the offer and acceptance. Whoever gives the woman in marriage should say: "Grateful praise to Allāh, and blessings upon Allāh's Messenger. I give you my daughter so-and-so in marriage."

The bridegroom should then say: "Grateful praise to Allāh, and blessings upon Allāh's Messenger. I accept her in marriage, on [the understanding that I shall provide] this dower." (The dower should be a definite and modest amount.) It is also commendable to praise Allāh before making the proposal of marriage.

iii) The bride should hear all about the bridegroom, even if she is a virgin; as well as being quite proper, this is conducive to greater harmony. It is likewise recommended that the groom should get to see the bride before the wedding, as this makes for better intimacy between the couple.

iv) It is good to invite other virtuous people, as well as the two witnesses whose presence is essential to the valid conclusion of the marriage contract.

v) The bridegroom should marry with the intention of upholding the Prophetic example, of preserving modesty, of seeking offspring, and of obtaining the other benefits we have mentioned above. His sole purpose should not be physical satisfaction and enjoyment, making his action an entirely worldly affair.

Not that these noble intentions are incompatible with such satisfaction, for duty may often coincide with desire; as 'Umar ibn 'Abd al-'Azīz[50] (may Allāh have mercy on him) said: "When duty coincides with desire, that is butter mixed with choice dates *[nirsiyān]*." It is by no means impossible for selfish satisfaction to motivate one along with a sense of religious duty.

vi) It is recommended, finally, that the marriage be contracted in the mosque and in the month of Shawwāl. 'Ā'isha (may Allāh be well pleased with her) said: "Allāh's Messenger (Allāh bless him and give him peace) married me in Shawwāl and also consummated our marriage in Shawwāl."

[50] 'Umar ibn 'Abd al-'Azīz ibn Marwān, the Umayyad Caliph (A.H 99–101). A man of piety and learning, he is renowned for his enlightened approach to government in a period of increasing worldliness.

The Bride

The prospective bride must be considered from two points of view: First, whether she can lawfully marry; second, the likelihood of a satisfactory married life and achievement of the purposes of marriage.

a) Conditions of legality

The woman must be free of impediments to marriage. These impediments are nineteen in number:

i. She is already married to another.

ii. She is in the period of withdrawal following widowhood, repudiation, or intercourse of uncertain legality. (Or, in the case of a slave-girl, she is in the period during which it is to be established whether or not she is pregnant.)

iii. She has become an apostate from Islām through having uttered a statement of unbelief.

iv. She is a Magian [Zoroastrian].

v. She is an idolatress or atheist *[zindīqa]*, owing allegiance to no Prophet or Scripture. (Included here are adherents of libertinism *[madhhab al-ibāḥa]*; marriage with them is unlawful, as it is with a woman belonging to any depraved sect whose members are regarded as unbelievers.)

vi. She is a woman of scriptural religion,[51] but embraced that religion after it had been falsified, or subsequent to the mission of Allāh's Messenger (Allāh bless him and give him peace). Furthermore, she is not an Israelite by birth.
(If she fails on both counts, it is definitely not permissible to marry her. There is disagreement as to whether she is disqualified by non-Israelite descent alone.)

[51] *Kitābiyya*, i.e., a Jewish or Christian woman.

vii. She is a slave, while the prospective husband is a free man, either capable of supporting a free woman, or [impoverished but] immune to moral danger [if he remains unmarried].

viii. She is wholly or partially owned as a slave by the prospective husband.

ix. She is closely related to the prospective husband, being an ascendant or descendant of his, a descendant of his ascendants in the first degree, or a descendant in the first degree of a more remote ascendant. By ascendant I mean mothers and grandmothers; by descendants of ascendants in the first degree, brothers and sisters and their children; by descendants in the first degree of any higher ascendants, I mean paternal and maternal aunts, but not their children.

x. She is forbidden through the relationship of suckling, which creates the same impediments as blood kinship with ascendants and descendants (see ix. above). However, no fewer than five acts of suckling are required to create this impediment.

xi. She is related to him through marriage, viz., (a) the prospective husband has already been married to her daughter or granddaughter; (b) he has previously acquired the latter by a contract of slavery, even if the contract is of doubtful validity; (c) he has had intercourse with these women due to a legal error in a contract; (d) he has had intercourse with her mother or one of her grandmothers, after a marriage contract or the semblance of one (the mere contract being enough to make it unlawful to marry her mother and higher ascendants, while her descendants are barred only if consummation has occurred); (e) she has previously been married to his father or son.

xii. She would be a fifth wife, i.e. the prospective husband already has four other wives, whether in the normal state of marriage, or in the period of suspension following a revocable divorce. (If one of the four is in the withdrawal period following an irrevocable repudiation, however, there is no impediment to his taking a 'fifth' wife.)

xiii. Her sister or her aunt (paternal or maternal) is already married to the prospective husband, so that he would be taking them both to wife at the same time. (This rule applies in all cases where two women are so related that, were one of them male, marriage between them would be unlawful.)

xiv. The prospective husband has thrice repudiated her. She is then unlawful to him as long as she has not consummated a valid marriage with a different husband.

xv. When the man has pronounced the oath of anathema *[liʿān]* against his wife, she is thereby forever unlawful to him.

xvi. Either party is in a state of consecration for the Pilgrimage or Visitation [to Mecca]; the marriage cannot be contracted till deconsecration has been completed.

xvii. She is a non-virgin minor; marriage with her is not valid until after she has attained puberty.

xviii. She is an orphan; marriage with her is not valid until after she has attained puberty.

xix. She was one of the wives of Allāh's Messenger (Allāh bless him and give him peace), and was left a widow by him, or he has cohabited with her; such women are 'Mothers of the Believers.' (This case is no longer relevant in our time, of course.)

So much for the impediments to lawful marriage.

b) Conditions of happiness

As for those qualities that make for a happy life, and which must be looked for in the woman so that the contract may prove durable and the object be achieved, these are eight in number: i. Religion; ii. Good character; iii. Beauty; iv. Moderate dower; v. Fertility; vi. Virginity; vii. Good lineage; viii. Absence of close kinship.

i. Religion

First and foremost, the bride should be a virtuous and religious woman; this is the fundamental consideration. If she is too weak in religion to protect herself and her womanhood, she will disgrace her husband, subject him to public humiliation, and trouble his heart with jealous feelings, so that his life will be in turmoil. If he turns to indignation and jealousy, he will suffer constant trial and tribulation;

if he turns to indulgence, he will neglect his religion and his honor, and be taken for a man lacking dignity and pride.

If she is not only corrupt but beautiful with it, the trouble she causes is even more intense, because her husband will find it hard to part with her. He cannot bear to be without her, yet her presence is unbearable. He is in the same predicament as the man who came to the Messenger (Allāh bless him and give him peace), saying: "Messenger of Allāh, I have a wife who does not repel the groper's hand."—"Divorce her!" said he.—"But I love her," the man protested.—"Then keep her!" said the Prophet (Allāh bless him and give him peace).

(He would hardly have given this last instruction unless he feared that, if the man divorced his wife, he would hanker after her and become corrupted along with her. He therefore thought it better that the marriage should continue, for all the pain it brought the husband, because it would save the latter from corruption.)

If the woman is so corrupt in her religion as to waste her husband's property, or in some other way to cause constant upheaval in his life, and he makes no complaint, then he becomes her accomplice in sin, contravening the Exalted One's words: "Guard yourselves and your families against a Fire..." (66:6). Yet if he complains and quarrels, his life becomes a misery.

That is why Allāh's Messenger (Allāh bless him and give him peace) went to great lengths in urging the choice of a religious wife, saying:

> A woman may be married for her fortune, her beauty, her lineage, or her religion. You must choose the religious one, or live to regret it!
>
> One who marries a woman for her wealth and beauty will be deprived of that wealth and beauty, but on one who marries her for her religion Allāh will bestow her wealth and beauty too.
>
> Do not marry a woman for her beauty, for her beauty may be the ruin of her; nor for her wealth, for her wealth may make her cruel. Marry a woman for her religion.

The reason for this great emphasis on religion is that such a wife will be an aid to religion, while if she is not religious she will distract her husband from his religion and be an annoyance to him.

ii. Good character

Second comes good character. This is an important element in the quest for peace of mind and help with one's religion. If a wife is impudent and foul-mouthed, of bad character and ungrateful for kindnesses, she will do more harm than good. Patience with the tongues of women is one of the trials borne by the Prophets.

An Arab once said: "Six kinds of women you should not marry: the *annāna*, the *mannāna*, the *ḥannāna*, the *ḥaddāqa*, the *barrāqa*, and the *shaddāqa*."

The *annāna* is one who does a lot of moaning and complaining, and is always bandaging her [aching] head. Marriage to an invalid or malingerer is no good at all.

The *mannāna* is one who always does things as a favor to her husband, then says: "I have done this or that for you!"

The *ḥannāna* is one who is always pining for a former husband, or for her child by a previous marriage. This is also something to be avoided.

The *ḥaddāqa* is one who covets everything on which her gaze alights, and who presses for husband to buy it.

For the *barrāqa* two meanings are possible: a) she spends the whole day long polishing her face and beautifying it to give it an artificial, lightning-like radiance *[barīq]*; b) she is always bad-tempered about food, will only eat alone, and always thinks her share of everything is too small; this is a Yemenite expression, used of a woman or child who is bad-tempered about food.

The *shaddāqa* is a talkative chatterbox, about whom the Prophet (Allāh bless him and give him peace) said:

> Allāh (Exalted is He) hates prattling chatterboxes.

It is related that the hermit of Azd[53] met Elias *[Ilyās]* (peace be upon him) in the course of his wanderings. The latter told him to marry, and forbade him to remain celibate; then he added: "Do not marry any of these four: the *mukhtali'a*, the *mubāriya*, the *'āhira*, and the *nāshiz*."

(The *mukhtali'a* is she who is always asking for a divorce *[khul']*[54] without a reason. The *mubāriya* is she who looks down on others, and takes pride in worldly things. The *'āhira* is the immoral woman known to have a sweetheart and lover; she is alluded to in the words of the

[53] Azd is the name of an Arab tribe. Bauer translates: 'der Wanderer von Ardan,' preferring the reading of the commentator Murtaḍā, and stating that Ardan is a watercourse in Syria. Bercher and Bousquet translate: 'l'ermite du Jourdain,' with the note: 'Sans doubte St. Jean-Baptiste; lire: *al-Urdannī*.'

[54] *khul'* is a form of divorce whereby the wife redeems herself from the marriage for a consideration.

Exalted One: "nor taking lovers" (4:25). The *nāshiz* is she who is overbearing toward her husband in word and deed.)[55]

ʿAlī (may Allāh be well pleased with him) used to say: "Three vices in a man are virtues in a woman: stinginess, vanity and timidity."

(If a woman is stingy, she will safeguard her own property and that of her husband. If she is vain, she will not condescend to engage in suspiciously tender conversation with just anybody. If she is timid, she will be scared of everything; she will not venture out of her house, and will avoid dubious places from fear of her husband.)

These reports draw attention to the sets of characteristics to be looked for in marriage.

iii. Beauty

Third comes beauty of countenance. This is also desirable as it is conducive to chastity, since a man's nature is not usually content with an ugly woman. Besides, physical and moral beauty normally go together. What we have cited to emphasize the importance of religion, and against marrying a woman for her beauty, should not be taken as a ban on giving beauty its due consideration, but as a caution against taking a wife for the sake of her beauty alone, regardless of the corruption of her faith. In most cases, in fact, it is beauty alone that makes marriage desirable, and the matter of religion is given little thought.

That attention should be paid to the beauty factor is proved by the fact that intimacy and affection usually derive from it, and the Sacred Law bids us respect the causes of harmony. This is why it is recommended that a prospective bride should be seen before marriage, for the Prophet (Allāh bless him and give him peace) said:

> When Allāh disposes one of you toward a woman, let him look upon her, for that is more likely to bring them close together.

(That is, to create intimacy between them.[56])

[55] The author notes that the root-word *nashaz* means 'high ground.'

[56] The author notes that the Arabic expression [*yu'dima bainahumā*] used by the Prophet (Allāh bless him and give him peace) suggests the contact of skin [*adama*] with skin. He explains that *adama* means the dermis or inner layer of skin, in contrast to *bashara*, the epidermis or outer layer, then adds that this expression must have been chosen to emphasize the degree of intimate harmony between the couple.

The Prophet (Allāh bless him and give him peace) once said:

> There is something about the eyes of the Anṣār.[57] So if one of you wishes to marry one of their womenfolk, let him look at them.

(Some say there was a bleariness in their eyes, while others maintain that they were small.)

Certain very pious men would only give their daughters in marriage if they had first been seen by their prospective husbands, as a precaution against illusion. Al-Aʿmash[58] said: "Every marriage that takes place without sight of the bride ends in sorrow and grief." Of course, everyone knows that visual inspection tells nothing about character, religion, or wealth, but serves only to distinguish beauty from ugliness.

It is reported that a certain man got married in the time of the ʿUmar (may Allāh be well pleased with him). Now this man had dyed his hair, and the dye later faded. The woman's family appealed against him to ʿUmar, saying: "We took him for a young man." ʿUmar had him beaten severely, saying: "You have deceived people!"

It is also reported that Bilāl[59] and Ṣuhaib approached some tent-dwelling Arabs and asked them for women in marriage. In reply to the question, "Who are you two?" Bilāl said: "I am Bilāl, and this is my brother Ṣuhaib. We were astray, but then Allāh guided us aright. We were slaves, then Allāh set us free. We were poor, then Allāh made us rich. If you give us wives—praise be to Allāh! If you reject us—glory be to Allāh!"

They said: "Of course you shall marry, and praise be to Allāh!" Then Ṣuhaib said to Bilāl: "You might have mentioned our exploits and our long service with Allāh's Messenger (Allāh bless him and give him peace)." But Bilāl replied: "Quiet! I spoke the truth, and truthfulness has got you married."

One may fall under illusion with regard to beauty and character alike. To dispel illusion in the former case, one is recommended to see for oneself; in the latter, to consult those who can give a description. This should be done in advance of the marriage. Enquiries about a woman's

[57] The 'Helpers', i.e., the people of Medina who came out in support of the Prophet (Allāh bless him and give him peace).

[58] Abū Muḥammad al-Aʿmash Sulaimān ibn Mihrān al-Kūfī (d. ca. A.H. 148). A famous Qur'ān-reader and narrator of Prophetic tradition.

[59] Bilāl al-Ḥabashī (d. A.H. 20). A slave of Abyssinian origin, he became the first Muezzin *[mu'adhdhin]* in Islām. May Allāh be well pleased with him.

character and beauty should only be made of someone who is perspicacious, truthful, aware of both outer and inner, not biased in her favor and so likely to praise her too highly, nor jealous of her and therefore grudging.

When marriage is in the offing, and it comes to describing marriageable women, human nature is inclined to exaggeration one way or the other, and few can give an honest and fair account. On the contrary, treachery and seduction are the general rule. Caution is vital in these matters for one who is afraid of being lured to the wrong wife.

As for the man whose purpose in taking a wife is to follow the noble Prophetic example, to have children, or to have his household managed, he will be closer to abstinence if he forgoes beauty. After all, it is in general a worldly factor, even if for certain individuals it can be an aid to religion.

Abū Sulaimān ad-Dārānī said: "Abstemiousness applies to everything, even one's choice of wife, so a man may marry an old woman because he prefers to abstain from the pleasures of this world."

Mālik ibn Dīnār[60] (may Allāh be well pleased with him) used to say: "One of you might refrain from marrying an orphan, although he would be rewarded for feeding and clothing her, and she would be inexpensive to maintain and content with little, preferring to wed the daughter of so-and-so (one of the sons of this world), who will beset him with her whims, saying: 'Get me this dress and that!'"

Aḥmad ibn Ḥanbal chose a one-eyed woman rather than her sister, although the sister was beautiful. He asked which was the more intelligent of the two. "The one with only one eye," they told him. "Marry me to her," said he.

Such is the conduct of those whose purpose is not sensual enjoyment. As for those whose religion is insecure unless they have the means to satisfy their desires, let them look for beauty. Taking pleasure in the permissible is a safeguard of religion.

As the saying goes: "When the woman is beautiful, of good character, black-pupilled, long-haired, fair-skinned, loving to her husband, keeping her glances for him, she is the very picture of wide-eyed houries."

That is how the women of Paradise are described by Allāh (Exalted is He) in His words: "Good and beautiful" (55:70)—by 'good', He means 'of good character'—and "Reserving their glances" (37:48; 38:52; 55:56), and "Amorous [*'urub*], coeval" (56:37; 78:33).

[60] Abū Yaḥyā Mālik ibn Dīnār as-Sāmī an-Nājī (d. A.H. 131). An ascetic and scholar.

(The word *ʿurub* is the plural of *ʿarūb*, which signifies a woman who is in love with her husband and has a craving for intercourse, thereby bringing delight to perfection. *Ḥawar* means whiteness, and *ḥawrā'* [hourie] designates a woman in whose eyes the white is intensely white, while the black is intensely black, like the blackness of her hair. The *ʿainā'* is a woman with wide eyes.)

The Prophet (Allāh bless him and give him peace) said:

> The best of your women is she who is pleased when her husband looks at her, who obeys him when he commands her, and who guards for him in his absence both herself and his property.

(The husband will only enjoy looking at her if she is a loving wife.)

iv. Moderate dower

In fourth place, the dower she demands should be moderate. As Allāh's Messenger (Allāh bless him and give him peace) once said:

> The best of wives are those with the prettiest faces, and whose dowers are least expensive.

He even forbade the giving of excessive dower.

The Messenger (Allāh bless him and give him peace) married one of his wives with a dower of ten dirhams and a set of tent furniture, viz., a hand-mill, a jar, and a leather cushion stuffed with palm fibers. For the marriage feast of one of his wives, he provided two measures of barley; for another, two measures of dates and two of *sawīq* [a gruel of parched barley].

ʿUmar (may Allāh be well pleased with him) also used to forbid excessively high dowers, saying: "Allāh's Messenger (Allāh bless him and give him peace) never married—nor gave his daughters in marriage—for more than four hundred dirhams."

Had it been a noble thing to provide women with huge dowers, Allāh's Messenger (Allāh bless him and give him peace) would have been the first to set an example of it. One of his Companions got married for a speck of gold worth five dirhams. Saʿīd ibn al-Musayyab[61] gave his daughter in marriage to Abū Huraira[62] (may Allāh be well

[61] Saʿīd ibn al-Musayyab [or, al-Musayyib] (d. A.H. 93). An early scholar of Prophetic tradition.

[62] Abū Huraira al-Dawsī al-Yamānī (d. A.H. 57–59). A Companion of the blessed Prophet. He transmitted an enormous body of tradition, and is held in high regard by the Ṣūfīs on account of his poverty and devotion.

pleased with him) for two dirhams, then he carried her to him in the night; he himself put her in at the door, then went away, returning to greet him a week later.

If one marries for ten dirhams (to be clear of amounts about which the scholars disagree), that is quite all right. According to one Prophetic tradition:

> The blessedness of a woman includes early marriage, prompt childbirth, and a modest dower.

The Prophet (Allāh bless him and give him peace) also said:

> The most blessed of them is she with the smallest dower.

Just as it is reprehensible for a woman to demand an exorbitant dower, so is it blameworthy on the man's part to make enquiries into her fortune. He ought not to marry from greed for wealth. As [Sufyān] ath-Thawrī[63] said: "If a bridegroom asks how much the woman owns, know him for a brigand."

If one makes a present to them [the women's relatives], it should not be given with a view to extracting even greater favors; the same applies in reverse. The intention to procure such advantage is a corrupt one. The exchange of gifts is recommended, however, for it gives rise to affection. The Prophet (Allāh bless him and give him peace) said:

> Exchange gifts and you will come to love one another.

The pursuit of increase comes under the words of Allāh (Exalted is He):

> Do not give seeking to multiply. (74:6)

(That is, do not give in order to ask for more.) It is also subject to His words:

> What you give at interest *[ribā]*, so that it will grow on people's wealth [does not grow at all with Allāh]. (30:39)

Ribā is [unfair] increase. What we are considering here, in short, is the pursuit of such increase, even in goods to which the law on usurious transactions does not apply. All this is reprehensible, and a blameworthy innovation in marriage, which turns it into a commercial deal and a gamble, and the true objects of which it corrupts.

[63] Abū 'Abdi'llāh Sufyān ibn Sa'īd [or Sa'd] ibn Masrūq ath-Thawrī al-Kūfī (d. A.H. 161). A scholarly ascetic, who founded a short-lived school of Islāmic jurisprudence.

v. Fertility

The fifth consideration is that the woman should be fertile. If she is known to be barren, one should refrain from marrying her The Prophet (Allāh bless him and give him peace) said:

> You should take a fertile and loving wife. If she has never had a husband and her condition is unknown, attention should be paid to her health and youth. Granted these two qualities, she is most likely to be fertile.

vi. Virginity

Sixthly, the woman should be a virgin. The Prophet (Allāh bless him and give him peace) said to Jābir, when the latter married a non-virgin:

> Why not a virgin for you to caress, and to caress you in turn?

Virginity confers three benefits:

a) She will love her husband and harmonize with him, and this will be conducive to affection. The Prophet (Allāh bless him and give him peace) said:

> You should take an affectionate wife.

Character is formed by familiarity with what one is first accustomed to. A woman who has come to know men, and had experience of different circumstances, may not be satisfied with certain attributes in her husband which conflict with what she has been used to, and so she may come to hate him.

b) It is calculated to perfect his affection for her, for a man is by nature somewhat averse from a woman who has been touched by another husband, and this may weigh upon his temperament whenever he recalls it. Some natures are more strongly affected than others by such aversion.

c) She will not pine for a former husband. The strongest love is generally that experienced with the first beloved.

vii. Good lineage

In seventh place, she should be of good pedigree, meaning that she should come of a religious and virtuous family, for she will have to raise her daughters and her sons; if not well brought up herself, she will not make a good job of their upbringing and training.

That is why the Prophet (Allāh bless him and give him peace) said:

> Beware of the greenery growing on the dung hill.

(When asked what he meant, he said: "A lovely woman of bad origin.") He also said:

> Choose well for your seed, because children tend to take after their mother.

viii. Absence of close kinship

The eighth consideration is that she should not be too closely related, since such closeness diminishes sexual ardor.

The Prophet (Allāh bless him and give him peace) said:

> Do not marry a very close relative, for the offspring will be feeble.

(That is to say, frail.)

The reason is that the effect [of close kinship] is to weaken passion. Passion is aroused by strong sensations of sight and touch, and they are strongly excited only by something strange and new. As for what is familiar, and has long been seen, it dulls the senses into incomplete perception and lack of excitement, so that desire is not kindled.

Such then are the qualitites to be sought after in a wife.

Qualities desirable in the husband

The marriage gûardian also has a duty to consider the qualities of the prospective husband. He should look to the interest of his precious one, and not give her in marriage to a man of poor physique or bad character, or who will fail to give her all her due, or who is not her equal in lineage.

The Prophet (Allāh bless him and give him peace) said:

> Marriage is a kind of servitude, so let each of you look to where he is placing his precious daughter.

This precaution is more important where she is concerned, because she is like a slave in marriage, and has no escape from it, whereas the husband always has the power of repudiation. Any man who marries his daughter to a tyrant or scoundrel or heretic or wine-drinker, offends against his religion and exposes himself to the wrath of Allāh, in that he violates a right of kinship and abuses his discretion.

A man said to al-Ḥasan: "Several suitors have asked for my daughter. To whom should I give her in marriage?" He replied: "To him who is aware of Allāh, for if he loves her he will respect her, and even if he comes to dislike her he will not be cruel to her."

The Prophet (Allāh bless him and give him peace) said:

> One who marries his precious daughter to a scoundrel violates his bond of kinship with her.

CHAPTER THREE

Conjugal Life

Duties of the Husband

It is the husband's duty to observe fair treatment and good conduct in twelve matters: i) the wedding feast; ii) companionship; iii) dalliance; iv) the exercise of authority; v) jealousy; vi) maintenance; vii) education; viii) distribution of time; ix) chastisement for disobedience; x) sexual intercourse; xi) producing children; xii) separation through repudiation.

i. The wedding feast is the first good custom to observe

It is a recommended practice. Anas[64] (may Allāh be well pleased with him) said: "Allāh's Messenger (Allāh bless him and give him peace) once saw a trace of yellow on ʿAbd ar-Raḥmān ibn ʿAwf[65] (may Allāh be well pleased with him). 'What is this?' he asked. He replied: 'I have married a woman for a date-stone's worth of gold.' To this the Prophet (Allāh bless him and give him peace) responded: 'Allāh bless you! Now give a wedding feast, even if it is just with a sheep.'"

On his marriage to Ṣafiyya, Allāh's Messenger (Allāh bless him and give him peace) himself gave a wedding feast consisting of dates and *sawīq*. He said:

> Providing this food is a duty on the first day; on the second it is a recommended practice *[sunna]*; on the third it is to get oneself talked about. If anyone wants to be heard of, Allāh will let everybody know about him [on the Day of Resurrection].

(This tradition is ascribed to the blessed Prophet only by Ziyād ibn ʿAbdi'llāh;[66] it is classed as uncommon *[gharīb]*.)

[64] Abū Ḥamza Anas ibn Mālik (d. A.H. 91–93). A prolific narrator of Prophetic tradition. He entered the service of the blessed Prophet when very young.

[65] One of the ten Companions to whom Paradise was promised. (The trace of yellow came from a perfume worn on festive occasions.)

[66] A traditionist from Kūfa (d. A.H. 183).

It is also commendable to congratulate the husband. On entering, one should say to the bridegroom: "Allāh's blessing for you and upon you. May He unite you in goodness!" The Abū Huraira (may Allāh be well pleased with him) relates that the Prophet (Allāh bless him and give him peace) ordained this.

It is further recommended that the marriage be made public. The Prophet (Allāh bless him and give him peace) once said:

> The difference between the lawful and the unlawful is the tambourine and the voice.

He also said:

> Publicize this marriage; celebrate it in the mosques; sound the tambourines to mark it.

Ar-Rubayyi', daughter of al-Mu'awwidh, is reported as saying: "Allāh's Messenger (Allāh bless him and give him peace) called upon me in the morning after my marriage was consummated. He sat on my bed while some slave-girls of ours beat the tambourine and sang eulogies of my ancestors slain in battle. Then one of them said: 'In our midst there is a Prophet who knows what tomorrow brings.' But he said to her: 'Do not speak like that. Go on with the tale you were telling before.'"

ii. Good treatment [of wives]—and putting up with annoyance from them, out of compassion for their intellectual limitations.

Allāh (Exalted is He) says:

> Be kind in compassion with them. (4:19)

Stressing their rights, He also says:

> They have taken from you a solemn covenant. (4:21)

Moreover, His words: "The companion by your side" (4:36), are said to refer to one's wife.

The last instructions given by Allāh's Messenger (Allāh bless him and give him peace) concern three things, about which he went on speaking till his tongue stammered and his words became incomprehensible. He started to say:

> The ritual prayer, the ritual prayer... and your slaves, do not impose on them what they cannot bear... Allāh, Allāh—remember Him where women are concerned, for they are captives [*'awānin*] in your hands.
>
> You have taken them as a trust from Allāh, and have treated their genitals as lawful to you by virtue of Allāh's word....

He also said:

> Whoever endures his wife's bad character, Allāh will give him a reward like that He gave Job for his tribulation, while to one who endures the bad character of her husband, Allāh will give a recompense like that of Āsiya, the wife of Pharaoh.[67]

You should know that treating them well means more than just keeping them from pain; it means putting up with the pain they cause, and forbearance with their uppishness and rages—following the example of Allāh's Messenger (Allāh bless him and give him peace). For his wives used to contradict him, and one of them nagged him from morning till night.

The venerable ʿUmar was once contradicted by his wife. "Will you contradict me, you wretch?" he cried. "The wives of Allāh's Messenger (Allāh bless him and give him peace) contradict him, and he is better than you," she replied, so ʿUmar said: "May [my daughter] Ḥafṣa suffer disappointment and loss if she contradicts him." Then he said to Ḥafṣa: "Do not be misled by ʿĀʾisha, the daughter of Abū Quḥāfa's son [Abū Bakr]. She is the darling of Allāh's Messenger (Allāh bless him and give him peace)." Thus he put her in fear of contradicting.

It is related that one of the wives of Allāh's Messenger (Allāh bless him and give him peace) pushed him in the chest, whereupon her mother tried to stop her. But the blessed Prophet said: "Let her be! They do worse than that."

An altercation once broke out between him and ʿĀʾisha, so they brought in the venerable Abū Bakr as a referee. He asked the Prophet (Allāh bless him and give him peace) to state his case, so the Messenger said to ʿĀʾisha: "Will you speak first, or shall I?" She said: "You go ahead, but speak only the truth." At this, Abū Bakr slapped her till her mouth bled, crying: "You little enemy to yourself! Would he tell anything but the truth?" She thereupon sought refuge with Allāh's Messenger (Allāh bless him and give him peace), crouching behind his back. The blessed Prophet said to Abū Bakr: "We did not invite you for this; this is not what we expected of you."

Another time, she spoke to him in these angry words: "You call yourself Allāh's Prophet indeed!" Allāh's blessed Messenger smiled, taking it with forbearance and good grace.

[67] The Lady Āsiya maintained her faith in the One Almighty God in the face of cruel torment.

He often said to her: "I can tell the difference between your anger and your good mood."—"How can you tell?" she asked.—"When you are in a good mood, you say: 'No, by the God of Muḥammad!' But when you are cross, you say: 'No, by the God of Abraham!'"—"You are right," said she, "because then I avoid your name."

It is said that the first love in Islām was that of the blessed Prophet for 'Ā'isha (may Allāh be well pleased with her).[68] He used to say to her: "I am to you like Abū Zar' to Umm Zar', except that I shall never divorce you."[69]

He used to say to his other wives:

> Do not torment me about 'Ā'isha! By Allāh, the Revelation never came down to me while I was in any bed but hers.

Anas (may Allāh be well pleased with him) said: "Allāh's blessed Messenger was the most compassionate of men toward women and children."

iii. Dalliance

A husband should not only put up with annoyance; he should also indulge in dalliance, fun and play, for this is what pleases the hearts of women. Allāh's blessed Messenger used to have fun with his wives, coming down to their intellectual level in his actions and manners. It is even related that he used to run races with 'Ā'isha. She would beat him one day, but when he beat her the next time he would say: "Tit for tat!"

Tradition tells us that Allāh's Messenger (Allāh bless him and give him peace) was the jolliest of men with his wives. 'Ā'isha (may Allāh be well pleased with her) said: "I once heard the voices of people from Abyssinia, and others, who were giving a performance on the day of 'Ashūrā.[70] Allāh's Messenger (Allāh bless him and give him peace) said to me: "Would you like to watch them play?" I said yes, so he sent for them and they came. Then Allāh's blessed Messenger stood in the doorway, placed one palm on the door, and held out his other hand. I rested my chin on his hand, and they began to play as I watched.

[68] Many traditions also testify to his love for his first wife, Khadīja (may Allāh be well pleased with her).

[69] Abū Zar' and his wife must have been a doting couple before his attentions strayed.

[70] The 10th of Muḥarram.

Allāh's Messenger (Allāh bless him and give him peace) started saying to me: "That's enough!", but I said: "Be quiet!"—two or three times. Then he said: "ʿĀʾisha, is that enough?" so I said: "Yes." He then signaled to them, and they went away."

Allāh's Messenger (Allāh bless him and give him peace) once said:

> The most perfect of the believers in faith is he who has the best character, and is most gentle toward his family.

He also said:

> The best of you is the best toward his wife, and I am the best of you toward my wives.

Tough as he was, the venerable ʿUmar said: "With his family, a man should be like a child. But when they turn to him for his knowledge, they should find him a man."

Luqmān[71] (may Allāh have mercy on him) said: "The wise man should be as a child with his family, but in public he should prove to be a man."

The words of the Prophet (Allāh bless him and give him peace): "Allāh loathes the *jaʿẓarī* and the *jawwāẓ*," have been interpreted as referring to one who is harsh to his family, and one who has a high opinion of himself.

This is also one of the meanings given to the word *ʿutull*, which occurs in the Qurʾān (68:13) in the sense of a man coarse of tongue and hard of heart toward his family.

Allāh's Messenger (Allāh bless him and give him peace) once said to Jābir:

> Why not marry a virgin? You will have fun with her, and she will have fun with you.

An Arab woman once described her late husband in these words: "By Allāh, he used to come in laughing and go out quietly; he used to eat whatever he found waiting for him, with no questions about what was lacking."

iv. Authority

In being playful, good-humored and compliant, a husband should not pamper his wife to such a degree as to spoil her character and make her

[71] Allāh (Exalted is He) has told us: "And We gave Luqmān wisdom." (31:12)

lose all respect for him. He should rather observe moderation in this, being ready to stand on his dignity and express displeasure whenever he sees something reprehensible. He should definitely not open the door to the encouragement of abomination. Indeed, if he ever sees something contrary to the Sacred Law, and to a man's sense of honor, he should growl like a tiger and roar like a lion.

Al-Ḥasan said: "If a man comes to pander to his wife's caprice, Allāh will topple him into the Fire."

'Umar (may Allāh be well pleased with him) once said: "Contradict women, for blessing lies in contradicting them." There is also a saying: "Ask their advice, and then do the opposite."

The Prophet (Allāh bless him and give him peace) said:

> Perish the slave of his wife!

He meant by this that if he acquiesces in her whims, he becomes her slave, and perishes. In fact, Allāh has put man in charge of woman, so for her to be in charge of him is a reversal of the natural order, and turns things upside down; it is obeying Satan, who said:

> And I shall command them to alter Allāh's creation. (4:119)

The man's proper role is to be leader, not led. Allāh calls men "overseers of women" (4:34), and He calls the husband a master, for the Exalted One says:

> They [Joseph and Pharaoh's wife] found her master at the door. (12:25)

But if the master turns out to be subservient, he "exchanges Allāh's favor for ingratitude." (14:28)

The woman's lower self is patterned after your own. If you slacken her reins a little, she will bolt off with you. If you loosen her bridle a span, she will drag you a yard. But if you restrain her, and tighten your grip on her when firmness is called for, you will keep her under control.

Ash-Shāfi'ī,[72] (may Allāh be well pleased with him) said: "There are three who will despise you if you honor them, but will honor you if you despise them: a woman, a servant and a peasant." (By this he meant: if you accord them nothing but honor, and do not blend harshness with gentleness, severity with kindness.)

[72] Abū 'Abdullāh Muḥammad ibn Idrīs ash-Shāfi'ī (d. A.H. 204). Eponym of one of the four schools of Islāmic jurisprudence (the Shāfi'ī school, to which al-Ghazālī belonged).

The wives of the desert Arabs used to teach their daughters to put their husbands to the test. A woman would say to her daughter: "Try your husband out first, before being bold and cheeky with him. Take away the tip of his spear; then, if he says nothing, use his shield to cut meat on; if he still says nothing, chop bones with his sword; if he takes even this without protest, put a pack-saddle on his back and ride him, for he is your donkey."

As a general rule, it is by moderation that the heavens and earth are kept in balance, and everything that exceeds its limit turns into its opposite. One should tread the middle path between contradiction and agreement, keeping to what is right in all this so as to be safe from their mischief, for "their guile is enormous" (12:28), and their spite is notorious, More often than not, they are of bad character and feeeble in intelligence, and the only way to compensate for this is by a blend of gentleness and authority.

The Prophet (Allāh bless him and give him peace) said:

> A virtuous woman stands out among other women like the *aʿṣam* crow among a hundred ordinary crows.

(*aʿṣam* means 'white-bellied.')

Luqmān gave this counsel to his son: "My son, beware of a bad woman, for she will turn you prematurely grey; beware of mischievous women, for they provoke one to no good; and be on your guard even with the best of them."

The Prophet (Allāh bless him and give him peace) said:

> Seek refuge with Allāh from three back-breakers.

(Among these he counted the bad wife, for it is she who turns a man grey before his time. It has also been said of her that "when you go to her, she insults you; when you go away, she betrays you.")

The Prophet (Allāh bless him and give him peace) called even the best women "the seducers of Joseph." By this he meant: "In preventing Abū Bakr from leading the prayers, you deviated capriciously from what was right."

When the wives of His Messenger divulged a secret of his, the Exalted One said:

> If you both [ʿĀ'isha and Ḥafṣa] repent, for your hearts have gone awry. (66:4)

('Gone awry' *[ṣaghat]* means the same as 'deviated' *[mālat]*.) Allāh said this about the best of the Prophet's wives!

The Prophet (Allāh bless him and give him peace) said:

> People ruled by a woman do not prosper.

'Umar (may Allāh be well pleased with him) once chided his wife for answering him back; he told her: "You are just a toy in the corner of the house. Unless we need you, you stay put."

There is indeed mischief in them, as well as weakness. Authority and sterness are the remedy for the mischief, while kindness and tenderness are prescribed for the weakness. A clever doctor is one who can suit the remedy to the sickness, so let a man first get to know his wife's character from experience, then give her the appropriate treatment according to the needs of her condition.

v. Observing moderation in jealousy

This means neither overlooking the symptoms of things that might have dire consequences, nor being unduly suspicious, looking for trouble and spying out secrets.

Allāh's Messenger (Allāh bless him and give him peace) forbade the "pursuit of women's private parts." (In another version, the expression is "catching women unawares.")

On his return from a journey, but before entering Medina, the blessed Messenger said:

> Do not call on women at night.

Two of his men disobeyed him and went on ahead. Each of them saw something he disapproved of when he got home.

According to a well known Prophetic tradition:

> A woman is like a rib; try to straighten it and you will break it, so leave it as it is, and enjoy the curvature.

This applies to the training of her character.

The Prophet (Allāh bless him and give him peace) once said:

> There is a jealousy which Allāh (Great and Glorious is He) abhors; namely a man's groundless jealousy of his wife, for that is a form of prejudice which has been forbidden to us, since "some suspicions are sinful. (49:12)"

'Alī (may Allāh be well pleased with him) said: "Do not be so suspicious of your wife that you get her a bad reputation." The proper kind of jealousy, however, is indispensable and even praiseworthy.

Allāh's Messenger (Allāh bless him and give him peace) said:

> The Exalted One is jealous, as is the believer. Allāh's jealousy is of a man's violating His prohibitions.

The Prophet (Allāh bless him and give him peace) also said:

> Do you marvel at the jealousy of Sa'd?[73] Allāh and I are more jealous than he, and Allāh is more jealous than I. Because of His jealousy, Allāh has forbidden abominations, apparent or concealed. Yet no one is more ready to accept excuses than Allāh; that is why He has sent warners and bringers of good tidings. There is none fonder of praise than Allāh; that is why He has promised Paradise.

Allāh's Messenger (Allāh bless him and give him peace) said:

> On the night of my Heavenly Ascension, I saw a palace in Paradise, and in its courtyard I saw a girl. "Whose palace is this?" I asked, and they told me it was 'Umar's. I wanted to look at the girl, but I remembered your jealousy, O 'Umar."

'Umar wept when he heard this, saying: "Could I be jealous of you, O Messenger of Allāh?"

Al-Ḥasan used to say: "Would you leave your women to be jostled by the louts in the bazaar? May Allāh disgrace the man who is not jealous."

The Prophet (Allāh bless him and give him peace) said:

> There is a form of jealousy that Allāh loves, and another form which He detests. The jealousy that Allāh loves is jealousy based on genuine misgivings, while the jealousy He loathes is that which is quite unfounded. The pride Allāh loves is that which a man has in himself in battle, and in his first clash of arms, while the pride He detests is vainglory.

The Prophet (Allāh bless him and give him peace) also said:

> I am a jealous man. There is no man who is not jealous, unless he is a freak.

The way to make jealousy redundant is by keeping wives inaccessible to male visitors, and not letting them frequent the markets. Allāh's blessed Messenger asked his daughter Fāṭima (peace be upon her): "What is best for a woman?"—"That she should not see a man, nor any man see her," she replied, whereupon he hugged her and said: "That's my daughter!" Thus did he show his approval of her words.

[73] Sa'd ibn 'Ubāda (d. A.H. 15). A Companion of the blessed Prophet.

The Companions of Allāh's blessed Messenger used to block up the skylights and vents, so that the women would not watch the men. Muʿādh once saw his wife looking through a skylight, so he beat her. He also beat his wife when he saw her give her slave boy an apple she had partly eaten.

ʿUmar (may Allāh be well pleased with him) said: "Let your wives have nothing nice to wear, then they will keep to their chambers." What he meant by this was that they will not care to go out shabbily dressed. He also said: "Let your wives get used to the word 'No!'"

Allāh's Messenger (Allāh bless him and give him peace) had allowed women to attend the mosque, but the right course nowadays is to prevent them from doing so, unless they are old. Indeed, this was already thought preferable in the time of the Companions; so much so that ʿĀʾisha (may Allāh be well pleased with her) said: "Had the blessed Prophet known what women would get up to after his death, he would have forbidden them to go out."

When Ibn ʿUmar said, "Allāh's Messenger (Allāh bless him and give him peace) said: 'Do not stop the handmaidens of Allāh from going to the mosques,'" one of his sons said: "By Allāh, we shall stop them!" The father then struck him in anger, saying: "You hear me tell you that Allāh's blessed Messenger said: 'Do not stop them,' yet you dare to say the opposite!" In fact, the son had only dared to contradict because he knew that times had changed; his father was angry with him only because he expressed his opinion so bluntly, with no apology.

Likewise, Allāh's Messenger (Allāh bless him and give him peace) had allowed the women to go out for certain festivals; even so, they only went out with their husbands' consent. Nowadays, it is permissible for the chaste woman to go out without her husband's consent, though staying at home is safer. She should only go out for something very important; sight-seeing or trivial excursions will jeopardize the husband's honor, and may lead to corruption. If she does venture out, she ought to lower her gaze from the sight of men.

(We are not saying that a man's face is an *ʿawra* [pudendum; private part] where she is concerned, as a woman's face is for a man; the comparison is rather to the face of a beardless youth in relation to a man. Looking is forbidden only when there is a danger of temptation, not otherwise, for men have always gone about with their faces uncovered, whereas women go out veiled. Had men's faces been *'awra* for women, men would have been commanded to veil themselves, or else women would have been forbidden to go out except in cases of necessity.)

vi. Moderation in maintenance

A husband should not be stingy in maintaining his wife, nor should he be extravagant; he should rather strike a balance.

Allāh (Exalted is He) says:

> Eat and drink, but do not be extravagant. (7:31)
>
> Do not keep your hand shackled to your neck, yet do not stretch it out too far. (17:29)

Allāh's Messenger (Allāh bless him and give him peace) said:

> The best of you is the best to his family.
>
> If you spend a dīnār in Allāh's cause, a dīnār to free a slave, a dīnār in alms for the poor, and a dīnār for your family, the most meritorious is the one you spend on your family.

'Alī (may Allāh be well pleased with him) is said to have bought each of his four wives a dirham's worth of meat every four days.

Al-Ḥasan (may Allāh be well pleased with him) said [of the early believers]: "They were bountiful in feeding their families, but spent little on furniture and clothes."

Ibn Sīrīn[74] said: "It is recommended that a man prepare for his wife a weekly dish of *fālūdhaj*."[75] (Providing sweetmeats might not seem too important, yet total neglect of this would constitute a miserly breach of good custom.)

The husband should instruct his wife to give away to the poor, as alms, any food which is left over and will not keep fresh. This is the lowest degree of charity; the wife should attend to it as occasion may demand, without her husband's explicit permission.

One ought not to keep a tasty dish to oneself, instead of sharing it with the family. That sort of thing causes bad feeling and is quite antisocial. If one is set on doing it, one should eat in secret, unnoticed by the family. Besides, one should spare them the description of anything one does not intend to let them eat. When the husband eats, the whole

[74] Abū Bakr Muḥammad ibn Sīrīn (d. A.H. 110). A pious scholar, renowned for his scrupulous accuracy in transmitting Prophetic traditions.

[75] A sweet made of flour and honey.

family should sit down at his table. The venerable Sufyān said: "I have heard that Allāh and His Angels bless a family that eats together."

The most important thing for a husband to observe in providing for his family is to feed them by legitimate means, and not to get into bad ways for their sake. The latter would be an offense against them, rather than consideration for them. We have cited Prophetic traditions on this point, when discussing the drawbacks of marriage.

vii. Education

A man who is getting married should learn about menstruation and its rules, so as to observe the necessary restraints. He should teach his wife the rules of ritual prayer, and about when prayers must or need not be made up by a woman in menstruation. For he is commanded to preserve her from the Fire, in the words of Allāh (Exalted is He):

> Guard yourselves and your families against a Fire.... (66:6)

He should instruct her in the beliefs of those who follow the Prophetic model, and should remove from her heart any innovation she may have heard of. He should instill the fear of Allāh in her if she is lax in the matter of religion.

He should teach her all that is necessary of the rules of menstruation and irregular bleeding, although the latter is a lengthy subject. The essential knowledge a woman must be given about menstruation concerns the prayers that are to be repeated.

When her bleeding stops just before the sunset prayer, if only by the time it would take to perform one prayer-cycle, she must make up the midday and afternoon prayers; if she stops by the same length of time before the morning prayer, then she must make up the [preceding] sunset and late evening prayers. This is the minimum that women observe.

If the husband is seeing to her instruction, she may not go out to consult the scholars. If the husband's own knowledge is inadequate, but he consults the Mufti on her behalf and conveys the reply back to her, again she may not go out.

Otherwise, she does not merely have the right to go out for consultation, but is duty-bound to do so, and it is a sin for the husband to stop her. Once she has learned her relgious obligations, she may not go out for a session of divine remembrance *[dhikr]* nor for extra studies, unless she has her husband's consent.

Whenever the wife neglects one of the rules governing menstruation and irregular bleeding, and the husband does not tell her about it, he is equally at fault and becomes her partner in sin.

viii. Equal treatment

If a man has several wives, he must treat them equally and not favor any of them. If he is going away on a journey and wants to take one of them along for company, he should draw lots among them. That is what Allāh's Messenger (Allāh bless him and give him peace) used to do. If he robs a wife of her night, he should make it up to her, as a religious duty. (In that case, he would need to know the rules of distribution of time, which are too long to mention here.)

Allāh's Messenger (Allāh bless him and give him peace) once said:

> He who has two wives, and favors one of them at the other's expense (or, in one version: "does not treat them equally"), will appear on the Day of Resurrection with one side of his body sloping.

Equal treatment applies only to gifts and to spending the night. Love and sexual intercourse are not subject to one's own volition. As the Exalted One said:

> You will never be able to treat your wives equally, even if you want to. (4:129)

That is to say, you will not treat them equally in respect of the heart's desire and the inclination of the soul, and from these follow differences in sexual matters.

Allāh's Messenger (Allāh bless him and give him peace) used to treat his wives equally in terms of gifts and spending his nights with them, but he said:

> O Allāh, this effort is within my power to make, but I am powerless over what You alone control (meaning: love).

ʿĀʾisha (may Allāh be well pleased with her) was the dearest to him of his wives, and the other wives knew this. During his final illness he was carried around, being moved each day and night so that he might spend a night with each of them. He would say: "Where am I tomorrow?" One of his wives understood what he really meant:

"All he wants to know is when will it be ʿĀʾisha's day?" They all said: "O Messenger of Allāh, we give you permission to stay in ʿĀʾisha's house, for it is painful for you to be transported every night." Said he: "Do you all agree to that?"—"Yes!"—"Then move me to ʿĀʾisha's house."

Whenever a co-wife gives her night to her companion, and the husband agrees, the right of the second is confirmed.

Allāh's Messenger (Allāh bless him and give him peace) used to apportion his time among his wives. He was proposing to divorce Sawda bint Zamaʿa, who was getting old, but she gave her night to ʿĀʾisha and asked him to let her keep the status of wife, so that she might be resurrected in the company of his wives. He then kept her as his wife, but did not allot her a night, giving ʿĀʾisha two nights and his other wives one night each.

Such was the excellent fairness and virility of the Prophet (Allāh bless him and give him peace), that when his soul yearned for one of his wives out of her turn, and he cohabited with her, he then made the rounds of all his other wives during the following day and night. We have it on the authority of ʿĀʾisha (may Allāh be well pleased with her) that Allāh's blessed Messenger went round all his wives in a single night. According to Anas, he went round his nine wives in one forenoon.

ix. Disobedience

Whenever a quarrel breaks out between a married couple and no settlement is reached (whether both sides are at fault, or only the man, with the wife unable to get the better of her husband, while he is unable to put her straight), then two arbitrators must be found, one from his family and one from hers, to examine their differences and effect a reconciliation.

> If they wish for a reconciliation, Allāh will put things right between them. (4:35)

ʿUmar (may Allāh be well pleased with him) once sent a referee to a couple, but he came back without having produced a settlement, so ʿUmar assailed him with his scourge, saying: "Allāh (Exalted is He) says: 'If they wish for a reconcilation, Allāh will put things right between them.'" The man went back again with a firm intention, coaxed them, and effected a settlement between them.

When it is purely a case of disobedience on the part of the wife, however, and since "men are set in authority over women" (4:34), the husband is entitled to correct her, and to bring her back to obedience by force. Likewise, if she is neglecting the ritual prayer, he has the right to compel her to perform it. However, he must approach this correction by degrees, beginning first of all with exhortation, admonition and threats, then if that is unavailing, turning his back on her in bed, or sleeping separately and shunning her even while sharing the same house with her. He may keep this up for one, two, or three nights.

If even this is of no avail, he may administer a beating calculated not to cause injury, not to break a bone, and not to make her body bleed. He may not strike her in the face, for that is forbidden.

Allāh's Messenger (Allāh bless him and give him peace) was once asked: "What is the wife's right against her husband?" He said:

> He must feed her when he feeds himself, and clothe her when he clothes himself. He must not disfigure her, and if he beats her he must do so without causing injury. He must not shun her except in bed.

He may be angry with her and shun her, when a matter of religion is involved, for up to ten days, twenty days, even a month. Allāh's Messenger (Allāh bless him and give him peace) did this when he had sent a present to Zainab and she had returned it to him. The wife in whose apartment he was [at the time] said: "She has treated you with contempt by returning your gift (i.e., humiliated and belittled you)." But the blessed Prophet replied: "You are too insignificant in the sight of Allāh to be able to humiliate me!" He then got angry with them all for a month, before going back to them.

x. Sexual etiquette

a) General observations:

It is recommended that the husband should start by invoking the name of Allāh (Exalted is He). Then, having first recited: "Say: 'God is One'" (112:1), he should proclaim the Supreme Greatness of Allāh and declare that none but He is worthy of worship. He should then say: "In the name of Allāh, All-High, All-Mighty. O Allāh, make it a good offspring, if You have decreed that one should issue from my loins."

The Prophet (Allāh bless him and give him peace) said:

> When one of you goes to his wife, saying: "O Allāh, turn Satan from me, and turn Satan from what You bestow upon us!", then if they conceive a child, Satan will not harm it."

When she is near the climax, say to yourself without moving your lips: "Praise be to Allāh, Who created man from water." (25:54)

One of the scholars of Prophetic tradition used to exclaim "*Allāhu Akbar!*" so loudly that the people in the house could hear his voice.

Further, one should turn away from the direction of Mecca, not facing in this direction during intercourse out of respect for the *Qibla*. The husband should cover himself and his wife with a garment.

Allāh's Messenger (Allāh bless him and give him peace) used to cover his head and lower his voice, saying to his wife: "Softly!"

According to one Prophetic tradition, he said:

> When one of you mates with his wife, let them not be naked like the ass and the she-ass (i.e., like a pair of donkeys).

The husband should begin with gentle coaxing and kissing. The Prophet (Allāh bless him and give him peace) once said:

> Let none of you fall upon his wife as an animal would do. Let there be an envoy between them.

When they asked: "What is this envoy, O Messenger of Allāh?" he replied:

> Kisses and sweet words.

The Prophet (Allāh bless him and give him peace) also said:

> Three things are weaknesses in a man: Meeting someone who wants to know him, but letting him go before learning his name and ancestry; secondly, rejecting the honor someone wishes to pay him; thirdly, approaching his concubine or his wife and taking her without first talking to her, caressing her and lying by her side, so that he uses her to satisfy his need before she satisfies her need through him.

Sexual relations are disapproved of on three nights of the month: the first, last and middle nights. On these nights, it is said, Satan is present at the coupling. It is also said that the devils mate on these nights. It is related that this disapproval has the authority of ʿAlī, Muʿāwiya and Abū Huraira (may Allāh be well pleased with them).

Some scholars recommend intercourse on Friday and the night before it, on the basis of the blessed Prophet's words:

> Allāh has mercy on one who copulates, then performs the major ablution.

(See Chapter V of the Book of Ritual Prayer.)

Then, when the husband has attained his desired end, let him attend patiently to his mate, until she also reaches her climax. It often happens that her orgasm is delayed, which further excites her passion; to withdraw from her at this point would cause her pain. The physical discrepancy in the matter of orgasm may cause mutual estrangement whenever the husband is too quick to ejaculate; simultaneity in the moment of orgasm is more delightful to her. The husband should not be preoccupied with his own satisfaction, because the woman will often be shy.

The husband should go to his wife once every four nights. This is fairest, because the [maximum permissible] number of wives is four.

One is therefore allowed to extend the interval up to this limit. It is best that the husband should increase or decrease the amount of intercourse in accordance with his wife's need to guard her virtue, since the preservation of her virtue is a duty of the husband. If the woman's claim on intercourse has not been fixed, this is because of the difficulty of making and satisfying such a claim.

The husband should not penetrate his wife during menstruation, nor after it is over until she has performed the major ablution. This is forbidden by an explicit text of the Book (2:222). It is also said to give rise to elephantiasis in the child so conceived. Otherwise, the husband may enjoy the whole body of the menstruating wife, except that he may not copulate ith her in the 'wrong place.'

Copulation with a menstruating woman is forbidden on account of noxiousness, and noxiousness always attaches to the 'wrong place.' Anal intercourse is therefore more strictly forbidden than normal copulation with a woman in menstruation.

(The Exalted One's words: "Go to your tillage as you wish" (2:223) mean "at any time you wish.")

The husband may use his wife's hands to masturbate, and may enjoy the region beneath her petticoat as he desires—short of actual copulation. During menstruation, the wife should wear a petticoat covering her from the groin to above the knee. This is part of good etiquette.

A man may keep company with his wife during her period, for eating, resting or other purposes, and he is not obliged to avoid her.

If the husband wishes to copulate a second time, having already done so once, let him wash his genitals first. If he has an involuntary nocturnal emission, he should not copulate until he has washed his genitals or urinated.

Intercourse is disapproved of during the early part of the night, lest one fall asleep in a state of ritual impurity. If one wishes to sleep or to eat, one should first perform the lesser ablution (the prayer ablution), for that is a recommended practice.

Ibn ʿUmar said: "I said to the Prophet (Allāh bless him and give him peace): 'May we sleep in a state of ritual impurity?' He replied: 'Yes, if you do the lesser ablution.'"

A relaxation of this is reported, however, for ʿĀʾisha (may Allāh be well pleased with her) said: "The Prophet (Allāh bless him and give him peace) used to go to sleep in a state of major ritual impurity, without touching water."

Whenever one goes back to bed, one should smooth the surface, or give it a shake, for there is no knowing what has happened to it in the meantime.

One should not have a haircut, cut the nails, shave, undergo bleeding, or part with any bit of oneself, while in a state of major ritual impurity; all these parts will be restored to one in the Hereafter, and one will then be impure at the Resurrection. It is said that every hair will ask one to account for its impurity.

b) Birth control:

It is good custom not to practice coitus interruptus [*ʿazl*], but rather to release the semen into the seed bed, i.e., the womb, for "there is no soul whose existence Allāh has decreed but will come into being," as Allāh's Messenger (Allāh bless him and give him peace) has said.

About the practice of *ʿazl*, the scholars are in disagreement as to whether it is permissible or blameworthy. There are four schools of thought: (i) That which permits it absolutely under all circumstances; (ii) that which forbids it under all conditions; (iii) the view that it is permissible with the wife's consent, but not without it; this view apparently forbids the detriment to the wife, rather than the *ʿazl* as such; (iv) the opinion that it is permissible with a slave-concubine, but not with a free wife.

The sound opinion, in our view, is that it is permissible. As for 'blameworthiness,' this term can apply to a ban tantamount to outright prohibition, or to a recommendation to abstain, or it can neglecting what is preferable.

'Azl is 'blameworthy' in this third sense, i.e., it involves neglect of what is preferable, just as it might be said that it is 'blameworthy' to sit in the mosque without occupying oneself with divine remembrance or ritual prayer, or that it is 'blameworthy' for someone who is present in Mecca as a resident not to perform the Pilgrimage every year.

What is meant by blameworthiness in this context is merely neglect of what is better and meritorious. This is confirmed by our explanation of the merit of having offspring, and by the words attributed to the Prophet (Allāh bless him and give him peace):

> A man should have intercourse with his wife, then he may be rewarded with a son who will fight and die [a martyr] in Allāh's cause.

By this he meant that the birth of such a son would come as a reward for the father, as the secondary cause [of his coming into being], although Allāh (Exalted is He) is his Creator and Vivifier, and it is He who gives him the strength to fight the Holy War. The man has played his part in the process of causation, by copulating so as to inseminate the womb.

When we say that there is no blameworthiness in the sense of a prohibition or recommendation to abstain, it is because prohibition can only be established either by a text or by an analogy based on a textual ruling. But there is no text, and no principle on which analogy could be based; or rather, there is indeed an analogical principle, as follows:

To abstain from marriage altogether, or to abstain from copulation after marriage, or to abstain from ejaculation after penetration, all constitute abstinence from what is preferable, but do not represent the infringement of a prohibition. There is no difference [in the case of *'azl]*, since the child comes into being from the sperm entering the womb as a result of four causes: marriage, then copulation, then continuing to the point of ejaculation, then remaining in position so that the sperm is deposited in the womb.

Some of these causes are more immediate than others. To prevent the fourth is like preventing the third, the third like the second, and the second like the first. None of this compares with abortion, nor with the live burial of a female child *[wa'd]*, which constitutes a crime against a being already in existence.

Existence itself comes by stages: The first stage of existence is when the sperm is deposited in the womb, mixes with the fluid of the woman, and is prepared to receive life; to destroy that is a crime. If it has developed into a clot, the offense is more serious. If the spirit has been infused into it, and its formation has been completed, the offense is more serious still. But the ultimate enormity is when the crime follows a live birth.

Our reason for stating that the first cause of existence is at the moment when the sperm is deposited in the womb, and not the moment when it leaves the urethra, is that the child is created not from the male sperm alone, but rather from the two spouses combined; either from his fluid and her fluid, or from his fluid and the menstrual blood.

Some anatomists maintain that the clot is created, by Allāh's decree, from the menstrual blood (this blood corresponding to the milk in curds, with the male sperm as the necessary condition for the coagulation and clotting of the menstrual blood, just as the rennet is needed for milk to thicken into curds.) However that may be, the woman's fluid is a basic element in the process.

The two fluids thus correspond to the offer and acceptance in the legal formation of contracts. If one makes an offer, but then withdraws it before acceptance takes place, there is no offense against the contract by way of annulment or abrogation. Once the offer has been matched with acceptance, however, withdrawal becomes a dissolution, an abrogation, and a breach. Just as a child cannot be created from the sperm in the man's spine, no more can it after leaving the urethra, as long as it has not mingled with the fluid of the woman, or with her blood. This is therefore the obvious analogy.

You may say: "But if *ʿazl* is not blameworthy in so far as it opposes the existence of a child, it may well be so by virtue of the intention that motivates it, since that intention can only be corrupt and tainted with concealed polytheism." To this I would reply that there are five possible intentions motivating *ʿazl*:

i. The first, which applies only to concubinage, is the desire to guard against the loss of property resulting from the right to emancipation [acquired by a concubine who bears her master's child]. But the aim of preserving property, by avoiding emancipation and opposing its cause, is not something forbidden.

ii. The desire to preserve a wife's beauty and natural plumpness for continued enjoyment, and to protect her life against the dangers of childbirth; this is not forbidden either.

iii. The fear of great hardship as a result of having too many children, plus taking precautions against the exhausting task of earning a livelihood, with its attendant involvement in improper activities; this also is not forbidden, since freedom from hardship is an aid to religious devotion. Of course, perfection and virtue lie in trust and confidence in Allāh's providence, for He says:

> There is no beast upon the earth for which Allāh does not provide (11:6)

Certainly, we have here a falling away from the pinnacle of perfection, and a neglect of what is more meritorious. However, to examine consequences, and to preserve and store up wealth, while perhaps at odds with the attitude of trust in Providence, cannot be called forbidden.

iv. The fear that having daughters to marry off may result in disgrace, which led to the pre-Islāmic Arab custom of killing female offspring. This is indeed a vile motive, and it is a sin to abstain from marriage or from sexual intercourse for this reason specifically. But the sin lies in the reason, not in the abstinence as such. The same applies to *ʿazl*.

The corruption is all the greater if one believes there is something shameful in a practice of Allāh's Messenger (Allāh bless him and give him peace). It is like the case of a woman who abstains from marrying because she is scornful of having a man above her, and who considers herself on a par with men. Here again, the blameworthiness does not attach to the refusal to marry in itself.

v. The woman refuses to have children because of her vanity, excessive concern with cleanliness, and reluctance to face childbirth, confinement and breast-feeding.

This was the custom among the women of the Khārijites,[76] who used excessive quantities of water, even made up the prayers of their days in menstruation, and would not go to the privy unless they were naked.

This is an innovation contrary to the Prophetic example, and therefore a perverse motive. One of those women sought an interview

[76] A secessionist group with extremist tendencies.

with ʿĀʾisha (may Allāh be well pleased with her), when she was staying in Baṣra, but she would not allow it. Once again, it is the intention that is wrong, not the refusal to bear children.

You may object: "But the Prophet (Allāh bless him and give him peace) said three times: 'Anyone who avoids marriage from fear of having a family is not one of us.'" But I shall reply: *ʿAzl* does resemble avoidance of marriage, but the blessed Prophet's words "is not one of us" signify: "He does not conform to our pattern and way of life, though our example is the worthier course."

Should you say, quoting a Prophetic tradition recorded in the *Ṣaḥīḥ* [of Muslim]: "But the blessed Prophet said of *ʿazl*: 'That is concealed *waʾd*,' reciting: 'When the girl child buried alive is asked...' (81:8)," I would reply that the same collection also contains genuine Prophetic traditions permitting it. The expression 'concealed *waʾd*' is like his other phrase, 'concealed *shirk* [polytheism]'; it implies disapproval, not prohibition.

Should you go on to say: "But Ibn ʿAbbās said: '*ʿAzl* is lesser *waʾd*, because the child whose existence is prevented is the lesser victim of *waʾd*,'" I would reply as follows: He draws an analogy between the prevention of existence and its extinction, but this is a weak analogy. That is why the venerable ʿAlī blamed him when he came to hear of it, saying: "There can be no *mawʾūda* [victim of *waʾd*] except after seven (phases of development)," and reciting the Qurʾānic verse about the phases of creation, in the Exalted One's words:

> We created man from purest clay, then placed him as a sperm-drop into a safe abode, then We brought him forth as another creation (i.e., breathed spirit into it). (23:12-14)

Then he went on to recite the Exalted One's words in the verse:

> And when the girl child buried alive is asked.... (81:8)

If you study what we have said above, by way of analogy and reasoning, it will be readily apparent to you what a great difference there is between the relative standing of ʿAlī and Ibn ʿAbbās (may Allāh be well pleased with them both) in ability to fathom meanings and to comprehend the sciences.

We also have the support of the generally accepted Prophetic tradition, reported in the two *Ṣaḥīḥ*'s on the authority of Jābir, who said:

"We used to practice *ʿazl* in the time of Allāh's blessed Messenger, while the Qur'ān was being revealed." (Or, in another version: "We used to practice *ʿazl*, and the blessed Prophet got to hear about it, but he did not forbid it.")

The following is also reported on Jābir's authority: "A man came to Allāh's blessed Messenger and said: 'I have a slave-girl who waits on us and waters our date-palms. I have intercourse with her, but I wouldn't like her to get pregnant.' The blessed Prophet said: 'Practice *ʿazl* if you wish, for whatever has been decreed for her will come her way.' Some time later, the man came to him again, saying: 'The slave-girl is pregnant.' Said he: 'I told you that whatever was decreed for her would come her way!'" (All this is in the two *Ṣaḥīḥ*'s.)[71]

xi. Having children

In connection with the birth of children, there are five proprieties to observe:

a) A man should not be too overjoyed at getting a boy, nor unduly sad at getting a girl, for he is not to know which of them will prove the greater blessing to him. How many fathers of sons wish they had none at all, or girls instead! Indeed, girls give more peace, and the reward they bring is more bountiful. The blessed Prophet said:

> If a man has a daughter, brings her up well, feeds her properly, and confers on her some of the bounties Allāh has bestowed on him, he has in her a guard to his right and a guard to his left—all the way from the Fire to the Garden of Paradise.

According to the venerable Ibn ʿAbbās, Allāh's blessed Messenger said:

> If any of you brings up two daughters, and treats them well as long as they are with him, they will admit him to Paradise.

Anas said that Allāh's blessed Messenger said:

> If anyone has two daughters, or two sisters, and treats them well while they are with him, he and I will be together in Paradise, like these two [fingers].

Anas also said that Allāh's blessed Messenger said:

> If anyone goes to a Muslim market, buys something, fetches it home, and gives it to the females rather than the males, Allāh will look upon him [with favor].

[77] Actually in the *Ṣaḥīḥ* of Muslim only.

From Anas again, we learn that Allāh's blessed Messenger said:

> If anyone brings his family a treat from the bazaars, it is as if he had brought them a charitable endowment; but let him start with the females before the males, for if one delights a female it is as if one had wept from the fear of Allāh, and if one weeps from the fear of Allāh, Allāh forbids one's body to the Fire.

According to Abū Huraira, Allāh's blessed Messenger said:

> If anyone has three daughters or sisters, and patiently endures hardship and distress on their account, Allāh will admit him to Paradise by virtue of his mercy toward them.

Somebody asked: "And two, O Messenger of Allāh?" — "And two," he replied. Then somebody asked: "Or one?" — "Even one," said he.

b) The second good custom is that one should give the Call to Prayer in the baby's ear.

According to Rāfi', his father[78] said: "I saw the blessed Prophet give the Call to Prayer in the ear of al-Ḥasan when Fāṭima (may Allāh be well pleased with her) had given birth to him."

The blessed Prophet is also reported as saying:

> If someone to whom a child is born gives the Call to Prayer in its right ear, and the *iqāma* [signal to begin the ritual prayer] in its left ear, Umm aṣ-Ṣibyān will be kept at bay.[79]

One is also recommended to teach the child to say "*Lā ilāha illa'llāh*" as soon as its tongue is loose, so that these will be its first words.[80]

Circumcision on the seventh day is recommended in a Prophetic tradition.

c) A fine name should be given, as something to which the child has a right.

Allāh's Messenger (Allāh bless him and give him peace) said:

> When you give a name, choose one beginning with 'Abd.
>
> Allāh's favorite names are 'Abdu'llāh and 'Abd ar-Raḥmān.[81]
>
> Give my name, but not my *kunya*.[82]

[78] Abū Rāfi', a protégé of the Prophet (Allāh bless him and give him peace).

[79] Umm aṣ-Ṣibyān ['Mother of Little Boys'] is variously interpreted as a malevolent spirit, flatulence, or elephantiasis.

[80] "There is none worthy of worship but Allāh."

[81] The names mean 'Servant of God' and 'Servant of the All-Merciful.'

[82] The *kunya* is a kind of agnomen, consisting of the word Abū [Father (of)...] or Umm [Mother (of...)] followed by the son's name.

(The scholars say that this applied in the blessed Prophet's own time, since people used to hail him with "Abu'l-Qāsim!", but that nowadays it does not matter. Anyway, one should not give both his name and *kunya* combined, since he said: "Do not give my name and *kunya* together," though some say that this also applied only in his own lifetime.)

One man was called Abū ʿĪsā ['Father of Jesus'], but the Prophet (Allāh bless him and give him peace) said disapprovingly: "Jesus had no father!"

The miscarried fetus should also be given a name. ʿAbd ar-Raḥmān ibn Yazīd ibn Muʿāwiya said: "I have heard that on the Day of Resurrection the miscarried fetus will cry after its father, saying: 'You have abandoned me and left me unnamed.'" ʿUmar ibn ʿAbd al-ʿAzīz said: "How could I give a name, not knowing if it was a boy or a girl?" But ʿAbd ar-Raḥmān replied: "There are names common to both sexes, such as Ḥamza, ʿAmāra, Ṭalḥa and ʿUtba."

The Prophet (Allāh bless him and give him peace) said:

> You will be summoned on the Day of Resurrection by your names and the names of your fathers, so be sure to give good names.

If someone has an unsuitable name, he is recommended to change it. Allāh's Messenger (Allāh bless him and give him peace) changed the name of al-ʿĀṣ to ʿAbdu'llāh. According to Abū Huraira, Zainab[83] was at first called Barra,[84] but the blessed Prophet said: "She attests her own probity."[85] He then renamed her Zainab.

It is likewise forbidden to use the names Aflaḥ [Lucky], Yasār [Prosperity], Nāfiʿ [Useful] and Baraka [Blessing], because one might ask: "Is Baraka there?" and get the answer: "No!"

d) The *ʿaqīqa*

This is the custom of sacrificing two sheep for a boy, and one for a girl (though it is all right to make it one sheep for either sex). We have it on the authority of ʿĀʾisha (may Allāh be well pleased with her) that Allāh's Messenger (Allāh bless him and give him peace) ordered the sacrifice—for a boy—of two sheep of equal value, and of one sheep for a girl.

83 Daughter of Abū Salama, a Companion of the blessed Prophet.

84 'Innocent'.

85 An allusion to Islāmic legal procedure: it is not for witnesses to attest their own probity.)

It is related that he sacrificed one sheep for al-Ḥasan; as a concession, therefore, one may sacrifice only one sheep [for a boy]. The Prophet (Allāh bless him and give him peace) said:

> With a boy there should be a sacrifice; so shed blood for him, and keep evil from him.

It is a good practice to give alms the weight of the child's hair in gold or silver. The blessed Prophet is reported as having told Fāṭima (peace be upon her), on the seventh day after the birth of Ḥusain, to shave his hair and give in alms the weight of his hair in silver.

ʿĀʾisha (may Allāh be well pleased with her) said: "No bone should be broken in the animal sacrificed as *ʿaqīqa*."

e) [Rubbing the child's palate]

The child's palate should be rubbed with a date or sweetmeat. Asmāʾ, daughter of Abū Bakr (may Allāh be well pleased with them both) is reported as saying:

"I gave birth to ʿAbdu'llāh ibn az-Zubair at Qubāʾ, then brought him to Allāh's Messenger (Allāh bless him and give him peace) and set him on his lap. He thereupon called for a date, chewed it, then spat [saliva] into his mouth. Thus the first thing to enter his belly was the saliva of Allāh's blessed Messenger. Having rubbed his palate with the date, he then prayed for him and blessed him. This was the first child born in Islām, and great was the rejoicing of the Muslims, because they had been told that the Jews had bewitched them so that they would never have children."

xii. Divorce

Divorce is permissible, but it is the most hateful to Allāh (Exalted is He) of all permitted things. It is only allowed, moreover, provided it is not associated with any unfair detriment. Whenever a man repudiates his wife, he causes her some harm, and it is not permissible to cause such harm to another unless there is an offense on her side, or compelling necessity on his.

The Exalted One said:

> If they obey you, do not seek a way against them. (4:34)

(That is to say, do not resort to some specious pretext for separation.)

If his father has an aversion to the daughter-in-law, the man should repudiate her. Ibn ʿUmar (may Allāh be well pleased with him) said: "I had a wife whom I loved, but my father hated her, and told me to divorce her. I consulted Allāh's Messenger (Allāh bless him and give him peace), who said: 'Ibn ʿUmar, divorce your wife.'"

This proves that the father's right is paramount, though on the assumption that, as in ʿUmar's case, the father's dislike is not malicious.

Whenever a wife causes harm to the husband, and humiliates his family, she is in the wrong. Likewise when she is of bad character or corrupt in religion.

Commenting on the Exalted One's words: "Do not expel them from their homes, and let them not go out from them, unless they have committed a flagrant offense" (65:1), Ibn Masʿūd said: "Whenever she humiliates his family and harms her husband, that is a flagrant offense." (While the Qur'ānic verse refers to the period of withdrawal [*ʿidda*], the point is still relevant here.)

If it is the husband who is in the wrong, the wife has the right to seek her freedom for a financial consideration. It is reprehensible for the husband to take from her more than [the dower] he has given—that would be an unfair exploitation of her, and would reduce the woman's sex to an object of commercial speculation.

The Exalted One says:

> It is no sin for the pair of them if she ransoms herself. (2:229)

The repayment of what she has received, or a lesser sum, is appropriate compensation.

If a wife asks for a divorce when there is nothing wrong, she commits a sin. As the Prophet (Allāh bless him and give him peace) said:

> A woman who asks her husband for a divorce, when nothing is wrong, will not smell the perfume of Paradise.

(Or: " Paradise is forbidden to her.")

According to another version of this Prophetic tradition:

> Women who go looking for a divorce are unsteady in their faith.

In divorcing a wife, the husband must observe these four points:

a) He should divorce her during a period of intermenstrual purity, in which he has not copulated with her. Repudiation during menstruation, or during a period of purity in which intercourse has taken place, is an unlawful innovation (even though it is effective in law), because it entails the prolongation of her *'idda*. If he does [repudiate her in this manner], he should take her back.

Ibn 'Umar once divorced his wife during menstruation, but the Prophet (Allāh bless him and give him peace) said to his father: "Tell him to take her back until she is clean, then menstruates, then is clean again. Then let him divorce her or keep her, as he wishes. That is the *'idda* Allāh has prescribed for divorcing wives."

(His reason for ordering him to wait for two periods of purity, after taking her back, was to ensure that the purpose of the recall would be more than just [correcting the procedure of] divorce.)

b) He should confine himself to a single repudiation pronouncement, and not use a three-in-one formula. A single repudiation followed by the *'idda* will achieve the purpose, while leaving open the possibility of taking her back during the delay, should he so wish.

If he utters a triple repudiation, however, he may come to regret it, and will then need to endure a long wait she she goes through an intervening marriage. Besides, it is forbidden for a man to contract a marriage with the intention of divorcing the woman so that she can again be lawful to her former husband, and the latter is implicated as the instigator of this illegality. His heart is attached to the wife of another (i.e., the wife of this *muḥallil*),[86] and he wants to see her divorced by him after a marriage of his own making. All this is bound to alienate the wife from him.

Such are the consequences of triple repudiation, whereas the single version is sufficiently effective without entailing anything unlawful. (I am not saying that triple repudiation is prohibited, but it is blameworthy on these grounds, and by blameworthiness I refer to neglect of one's own best interest.)

c) The husband should be gentle in giving his reasons for repudiating her. He should avoid unkindness and belittlement, and should soothe her heart with a present, by way of consolation and reparation for the distress the divorce must cause her.

[86] The technical term for a man who marries a triply divorced woman in order to render her lawful in due course to her former husband.

The Exalted One said:

Compensate them! (33:49)

(This is obligatory whenever the marriage was originally contracted without the amount of the dower being stipulated.)

ʿAlī's son al-Ḥasan (may Allāh be well pleased with them both) was an habitual divorcer and marrier. One day, he sent a companion of his to tell two of his wives that he was divorcing them. He said: "Tell them to observe the *ʿidda*," and instructed him to give each of them ten thousand dirhams. The companion carried out these instructions. On his return, he was asked what they had done. "One of them bowed her head and said nothing. The other wept and wailed, and I heard her say: 'Small recompense for a loved one leaving.'" When al-Ḥasan heard this, he hung his head and felt sorry for her. He said: "If I were ever to take a woman back after divorcing her, it would be her."

One day, al-Ḥasan visited ʿAbd ar-Raḥmān ibn al-Ḥārith ibn Hishām, the chief of the scholars of Medina, where he had no peer.

(It was to him that ʿĀʾisha [may Allāh be well pleased with her] referred when she said: "Not to have embarked on that journey of mine would have been dearer to me than to have had sixteen sons by Allāh's blessed Messenger, all of them like ʿAbd ar-Raḥmān ibn al-Ḥārith ibn Hishām.")

Al-Ḥasan entered his house, and ʿAbd ar-Raḥmān received him with honor, seated him in his place and said: "Why didn't you send for me? I would have come to you." — "I need something from you," said al-Ḥasan.—"What is it?"—"I have come to you as a suitor for your daughter."

ʿAbd ar-Raḥmān lowered his head, then he looked up as he said: "By Allāh, no other person walking this earth is dearer to me than you. But, you know, my daughter is part of me; what hurts her, hurts me; what makes her happy, makes me happy too. As you are a confirmed divorcer, I am afraid that you may divorce her. Should you do that, I fear that my love for you might change. I should hate to have my heart turn against you, for you are a part of Allāh's Messenger (Allāh bless him and give him peace). If you promise not to repudiate her, I will give her to you in marriage."

Al-Ḥasan made no reply, but got up and left. According to a member of his household, he was heard to say as he was leaving: "What ʿAbd ar-Raḥmān wanted was nothing less than to make his daughter a collar around my neck!"

'Alī (may Allāh be well pleased with him) was very upset about Ḥasan's numerous divorces. He complained about them from the pulpit, saying in one of his sermons: "Ḥasan is a great divorcer, so do not give him your daughters in marriage." But up jumped a man of the tribe of Hamdān, who cried: "By Allāh, O Commander of the Believers, we shall give him our daughters in marriage as much as he wishes. If he pleases he may keep his wives, and if he wishes he may abandon them." This pleased 'Alī, who said: "If I were a gate-keeper of Paradise, I would say to the tribe of Hamdān: 'Enter in peace!'"

This makes the point that when someone blames a beloved spouse or child, from some feeling of shame, one ought not to support him, for it would be bad to do so. Good custom demands that one should contradict the person concerned as much as possible, because this will please his heart, and will conform more closely to his real inner feeling.

The purpose of all this is to demonstrate that divorce is permissible. Allāh (Exalted is He) has promised enrichment in divorce and in marriage alike, saying:

> Give in marriage those among you who are unattached, and the pious among your slaves and maidservants. If they are poor, Allāh will enrich them from His bounty. (24:32)

and:

> If they separate, Allāh will provide for each of them out of His abundance. (4:130)

d) The husband should not reveal secrets about his wife, no more after a repudiation than during the marriage itself. Authentic tradition reports dreadful threats levelled at those who reveal women's secrets.

It is related about a certain virtuous man that he wanted to divorce a wife, so he was asked: "What have you against her?" He replied: "A man of understanding does not reveal the secret of his wife." After the divorce, he was asked why he had divorced her, but he said: "What business of mine is another man's wife?"

We have now explained the duties incumbent on the husband.

Rights of the Husband

It is enough to say that marriage is a kind of slavery, for a wife is a slave to her husband. She owes her husband absolute obedience in whatever he may demand of her, where she herself is concerned, as long as no sin is involved. We find many traditions emphasizing the husband's right over his wife.

The Prophet (Allāh bless him and give him peace) has said:

> A woman who dies, leaving her husband content with her, will enter Paradise.

A man, who was going on a journey, once made his wife promise that she would not come downstairs from the upper quarters. Now her father lived downstairs, and he fell sick. The woman therefore sent to Allāh's Messenger (Allāh bless him and give him peace) to ask permission to go down to her father. The blessed Prophet said: "Obey your husband!" Then her father died, so she asked again, but again he said: "Obey your husband!" Then her father was buried. Allāh's blessed Messenger sent word to her that God had forgiven her father on account of her obedience to her husband.

The Prophet (Allāh bless him and give him peace) said:

> If a woman prays her five prayers, fasts during the month of Ramaḍān, guards her genitals, and obeys her husband, she will enter Paradise.

He thus associated obedience to the husband with the fundamentals of Islām.

The Prophet (Allāh bless him and give him peace) once said of women:

> Those who carry children, give birth to them, feed them at the breast, and treat them kindly—as long as they do nothing against their husbands—will, if they do their prayers, go to Paradise.

The Prophet (Allāh bless him and give him peace) also said:

> I once looked into the Fire, and saw that most of the people there were women.

Some women then asked: "O Messenger of Allāh, why?" He then replied: "They cursed a lot, and were ungrateful to their companion (i.e., the husband in whose company they lived)."

According to another Prophetic tradition:

> I looked into Paradise, and saw that women were in a minority there. I asked: 'Where are the women?'—'They are distracted by the two red things, gold and saffron (i.e., jewelry and dyed clothes).'

'Ā'isha (may Allāh be well pleased with her) said: "A young woman once came to the blessed Prophet and said: 'Messenger of Allāh, I am a young woman who receives proposals, but I find marriage distasteful. What is the husband's right over the wife?' He said: 'If he was sore from head to foot and she licked him, she would not have discharged her debt of gratitude.'—'Then I should not marry?' said she. But he replied: 'Oh yes, get married, for that is best.'"

According to Ibn 'Abbās, a woman of the tribe of Khath'am came to the Prophet (Allāh bless him and give him peace), saying: "I am a woman without a husband, and I want to get married. What right does the husband have?" He replied:

> One right of the husband over the wife is that if he should desire her, and seek to seduce her, even if she is on the back of a camel she should not refuse him. It is also his right that she should not give away anything from his house without his permission, for if she does this the guilt is upon her, while he will get the reward. Another right of his is that she should not perform supererogatory fasting without his permission, for if she does it, she will feel hunger and thirst, but the fast will not be accepted of her. If she goes out of the house without his permission, the angels will curse her until she returns home or repents.

The Prophet (Allāh bless him and give him peace) said:

> Were I to order anyone to prostrate before another, I would order the wife to prostrate herself before her husband, so great is his right over her.
>
> A woman is closest to the face of her Lord when she is inside her house. The prayer she performs in the courtyard of her house is more meritorious than the prayer she performs in the mosque, while her prayer in her apartment is more meritorious than her prayer in the courtyard of her house, and her prayer in her inner chamber is more meritorious than her prayer in her apartment.

That is because it is more private. This is why the Prophet (Allāh bless him and give him peace) said:

> A woman is nakedness, so when she goes out, the devil gets up to look at her.

> Woman has ten nakednesses. When she gets married, her husband veils one of them; when she dies, the grave veils all ten.

The husband's rights over his wife are therefore many. The most important of them are two: First, chastity and modesty; secondly, not making unnecessary demands upon him, and having nothing to do with any illegal income of his. Such was the custom of the women in the early days of Islām. When a man went out of his house, his wife and daughters would say to him: "Beware of illegal earning, for we can bear hunger and hardship, but we cannot endure the Fire."

One of the early believers planned to go on a journey, but his neighbors disapproved of his traveling. They said to his wife: "Why do you agree to his going on a journey, when he is leaving nothing to support you?" Said she: "As long as I have known my husband, I have known him as a consumer, not as a provider. I have a Provident Lord. The consumer is going away, but the Provider will remain."

Rābiʿa bint Ismāʿīl asked Aḥmad ibn Abi'l-Ḥawārī[87] to marry her, but he did not like the idea on account of his deep involvement in religious exercises. He said to her: "I have no concern with women, on account of my preoccupation with my own spiritual state." To this she replied: "I am more concerned with my own spiritual state than you with yours. Nor do I have any physical desire. However, I have inherited considerable wealth from my late husband, so I was wanting you to spend it on your brothers. Through you, I should get to know righteous people, and this would be for me a path leading to Allāh (Magnified and Glorified is He)."

He said: "I must first ask the permission of my master." Then he went to look for Abū Sulaimān ad-Dārānī, who had previously forbidden him to marry, saying: "Not one of our companions has married without changing for the worse." But when he heard what the lady had said, he said: "Marry her, for she is a friend of Allāh. This is the speech of the true saints."

Aḥmad continued: "So I married her. Now in our house there was a nook of plaster, which was destroyed by the hand-washing of people hurrying out after eating, apart from those who washed with potash. In addition to her, I married three other wives. She also fed me well, and used to perfume me. She would say: 'Go with full vigor and strength to your wives!'"

[87] A respected Syrian Ṣūfī of the second Islāmic century.

(This Rābiʿa occupied a position among the Syrians rather like that of Rābiʿa al-ʿAdawiyya[88] in Baṣra.)

One of the wife's duties is not to squander her husband's wealth, but to take care of it. Allāh's Messenger (Allāh bless him and give him peace) said:

> She is not permitted to give away food from his house without his permission, except for fresh food in danger of going bad. If she gives food with his consent, she gets the reward just as he does, but if she gives away food without his permission, he gets the reward while she bears the burden of sin.

One of a woman's rights over her parents is instruction in good companionship, and the manners and customs of living together with the husband. Thus it is related that Asmāʾ bint Khārija al-Fazārī said to her daughter on the occasion of her marriage: "You are leaving the nest in which you have grown up, for a bed unknown to you, beside a spouse who is a stranger to you. Be an earth for him, and he will be a sky for you; be a pillar for him, and he will be a support for you; be a servant for him, and he will be a slave for you. Do not trouble him, for he will hate you; do not go away from him, for he will forget you. If he approaches you, draw close to him, but if he keeps his distance from you, keep your distance from him. Look after his senses of smell, hearing and sight, so that from you he will always smell sweetness, hear pleasantness, and see what is beautiful."

A man once said to his wife:

> Take what I have to spare, and make my love last.
> Don't speak to me when with anger I am enraged.
> Never drum on me like on your tambourine.
> If you do, you may find yourself unengaged.
>
> Don't complain too much, or you'll chase away passion;
> My heart may reject you—hearts cannot be caged.
> I once saw love sharing the same heart with pain,
> But then love's departure was hastily staged.

To sum up briefly the proprieties to be observed by a wife:

She should stay inside her house, and stick to her spinning wheel. She should not go up too often to the roof and look around. She should talk little with the neighbors, and visit them only when it is really necessary to do so. She should look after the interests of her spouse in his absence and in his presence, seeking to please him in all that she does. She must

[88] A remarkable saint and mystic, devoted to loving intimacy with Allāh (Exalted is He). She died in A.H. 185.

be loyal to him in respect of herself and of her property. She should not go out of her house without his permission. When she does go out with his permission, she should be disguised in shabby attire, keeping to out-of-the-way places far from the main streets and markets. She should be careful not to let a stranger hear her voice or recognize her by her shape. While she is about her business she ought not to disclose her identity to her husband's friends; indeed, she should avoid recognition by anyone who thinks he knows her, or whom she recognizes.

Her only concern should be to keep things right and to manage her household. She should be diligent in observing her prayer and fasting. Should a friend of her husband come to the door and ask to be let in, while the husband is absent, she ought not to question him or engage him in conversation. She must jealously guard her own virtue and her husband's honor. She should be satisfied with the provision Allāh has bestowed upon her husband. She should always put her husband's rights before her own and those of her relatives. She should keep herself clean, and be ready under all circumstances for him to enjoy her if he wishes. She should be kind to her children and careful to protect them. She ought to hold her tongue from swearing at the children and contradicting her husband.

The Prophet (Allāh bless him and give him peace) once said:

> I and a woman with sunburned cheeks will go to Paradise, like these two [fingers]: A woman who was widowed by her husband, then kept herself for her daughters until they experienced marriage or died.

The Prophet (Allāh bless him and give him peace) also said:

> Allāh has forbidden any human being to enter Paradise before me, and yet I looked to my right and saw a woman hurrying on ahead of me to the gate of Paradise. I said: "How is it that this woman is going ahead of me?" The answer came: "O Muḥammad, this woman was kind and beautiful; she had with her daughters orphaned by her late husband. She looked after them patiently until they were well established, and now Allāh has rewarded her in this fashion.

Good manners demand that the wife should not boast of her beauty at the husband's expense, nor mock him for his ugliness. It is related that al-Aṣmaʿī[89] said:

"I went into the desert and there I happened to see an exceptionally good looking woman married to an extraordinarily ugly man. So I said to her: 'O ..., can you be content to be married to somebody like that?'

[89] Abū Saʿīd ʿAbd al-Malik ibn Quraib al-Aṣmaʿī (d. A.H. 213). A famous Arabic philologist.

To this she replied: 'Be quiet, will you! What you are saying is bad. Perhaps he has done well in relation to his Creator, so that He has made me his reward, or maybe I have done badly in relation to my Creator, so that He has made him my punishment. Surely I should be content with what Allāh has seen fit for me.' Thus she left me speechless."

Al-Aṣma'ī also relates:

"I once saw among the Bedouin a woman wearing a red skirt and made up with dye, carrying prayerbeads in her hand. 'How incongruous!' said I. But she said: 'I do not neglect my duty to Allāh, but fun and games are my duty too.' Then I realized that she was a virtuous woman with a husband for whom she was adorning herself."

Good custom also requires that a wife should observe correct conduct and remain subdued during the absence of her husband. Once he has returned, however, she should get back to playfulness, relaxation and everything that gives pleasure. She ought not to annoy her husband in any way. Mu'ādh ibn Jabal is reported as saying that Allāh's Messenger (Allāh bless him and give him peace) said:

> A wife had better not annoy her husband in this world, otherwise his wife among the wide-eyed houries will say: "Do not annoy him—may Allāh be your enemy—for he is only a guest with you, and will soon leave you to join us."

One of the duties of marriage incumbent on the wife is that when her husband dies, she should mourn him for no more than four months and ten days, during which time she should forsake perfumes and ornaments. Zainab bint Abī Salama[90] said:

"I once visited Umm Ḥabība, the wife of the Prophet (Allāh bless him and give him peace), when her father Abū Sufyān ibn Ḥarb[91] had died. She called for a perfume with yellow in it, *khalūq*, or some other, with which she first anointed her servant-girl, then applied it to her own cheeks. Then she said: 'By Allāh, it is not that I have any need of perfume, but I heard Allāh's Messenger (Allāh bless him and give him peace) say: "It is not permissible for a woman who believes in Allāh and the Last Day to stay in mourning longer than three days, except for a husband, when it is four months and ten days."'"

[90] See n. 83 on p. 83 above.

[91] Abū Sufyān ibn Ḥarb ibn Umayya (d. ca. A.H. 32). A prominent Meccan merchant and financier, who was a leading opponent of the blessed Prophet in the early days. He eventually submitted, and helped to bring about the peaceful surrender of Mecca.

A further duty of the wife is to stay in the conjugal home until the end of the *ʿidda* period, during which time she may not move to her family home, nor go out except in case of real necessity.

It is good custom also for her to take charge of every household service of which she is capable. It is related of Asmāʾ the daughter of Abū Bakr the Truthful (may Allāh be well pleased with them both) that she said:

"When az-Zubair[92] married me, he had on this earth neither property nor slaves, in fact nothing at all except a horse and a water-bearing camel. I used to give his horse its fodder, care for it and groom it, and I used to crush date-stones for his water-camel and give it its fodder and draw water with it. I used to sew up his leather bottle and knead dough. I used to carry date-stones on my head for two-thirds of a league. Eventually Abū Bakr sent me a servant girl, who took over the grooming of the horse. It was as if I had been emancipated!

"One day I met Allāh's Messenger (Allāh bless him and give him peace) together with his companions, as I was carrying date-stones on my head. The blessed Prophet said: '*Ikh, ikh!*' to make his camel kneel and pick me up behind him. But I was ashamed to ride with the men, and thought of az-Zubair and his jealousy, for he was the most jealous of men. Allāh's blessed Messenger realized that I felt ashamed. So I came to az-Zubair and told him what had happened, and he said: 'By Allāh, your having to carry date-stones on your head is harder for me to bear than your riding with him.'"

The book of the proprieties of marriage ends here, with praise to Allāh and thanks for His bounty. Allāh's blessings upon every chosen creature.

[92] Az-Zubair ibn al-ʿAwwām (d. A.H. 36). A cousin of the Prophet (Allāh bless him and give him peace), and one of the earliest believers.

About the Translator

Muhtar Holland was born in 1935, in the ancient city of Durham in the North East of England. This statement may be considered anachronistic, however, since he did not bear the name Muhtar until 1969, when he was moved—by powerful experiences in the *latihan kejiwaan* of Subud—to embrace the religion of Islām.*

At the age of four, according to an entry in his father's diary, he said to a man who asked his name: "I'm a stranger to myself." During his years at school, he was drawn most strongly to the study of languages, which seemed to offer signposts to guide the stranger on his "Journey Home," apart from their practical usefulness to one who loved to spend his vacations traveling—at first on a bicycle—through foreign lands. Serious courses in Latin, Greek, French, Spanish and Danish, with additional smatterings of Anglo-Saxon, Italian, German and Dutch. Travels in France, Germany, Belgium, Holland and Denmark. Then a State Scholarship and up to Balliol College, Oxford, for a degree course centered on the study of Arabic and Turkish. Travels in Turkey and Syria. Then National Service in the Royal Navy, with most of the two years spent on an intensive course in the Russian language.

In the years since graduation from Oxford and Her Majesty's Senior Service, Mr. Holland has held academic posts at the University of Toronto, Canada; at the School of Oriental and African Studies in the University of London, England (with a five-month leave to study Islamic Law in Cairo, Egypt); and at the Universiti Kebangsaan in Kuala Lumpur, Malaysia (followed by a six-month sojourn in Indonesia). He also worked as Senior Research Fellow at the Islamic Foundation in Leicester, England, and as Director of the Nūr al-Islām Translation Center in Valley Cottage, New York.

* The name Muhtar was received at that time from Bapak Muhammad Subuh Sumohadiwidjojo, of Wisma Subud, Jakarta, in response to a request for a suitable Muslim name. In strict academic transliteration from the Arabic, the spelling would be *Mukhtār*. The form *Muchtar* is probably more common in Indonesia than *Muhtar*, which happens to coincide with the modern Turkish spelling of the name.

His freelance activities have mostly been devoted to writing and translating in various parts of the world, including Scotland and California. He made his Pilgrimage *[Ḥajj]* to Mecca in 1980.

Published works include the following:

Al-Ghazālī. *On the Duties of Brotherhood*. Translated from the Classical Arabic by Muhtar Holland. London: Latimer New Dimensions, 1975. New York: Overlook Press, 1977. Repr. 1980 and 1993.

Sheikh Muzaffer Ozak al-Jerrahi. *The Unveiling of Love*. Translated from the Turkish by Muhtar Holland. New York: Inner Traditions, 1981. Westport, Ct.: Pir Publications, 1990.

Ibn Taymīya. *Public Duties in Islām*. Translated from the Arabic by Muhtar Holland. Leicester, England: Islamic Foundation, 1982.

Hasan Shushud. *Masters of Wisdom of Central Asia*. Translated from the Turkish by Muhtar Holland. Ellingstring, England: Coombe Springs Press, 1983.

Al-Ghazālī. *Inner Dimensions of Islamic Worship*. Translated from the Arabic by Muhtar Holland. Leicester, England: Islamic Foundation, 1983.

Sheikh Muzaffer Ozak al-Jerrahi. *Irshād*. Translated [from the Turkish] with an Introduction by Muhtar Holland. Warwick, New York: Amity House, 1988. Westport, Ct.: Pir Publications, 1990.

Sheikh Muzaffer Ozak al-Jerrahi. *Blessed Virgin Mary*. Translation from the original Turkish by Muhtar Holland. Westport, Ct.: Pir Publications, 1991.

Sheikh Muzaffer Ozak al-Jerrahi. *The Garden of Dervishes*. Translation from the original Turkish by Muhtar Holland. Westport, Ct.: Pir Publications, 1991.

Sheikh Muzaffer Ozak al-Jerrahi. *Adornment of Hearts*. Translation from the original Turkish by Muhtar Holland and Sixtina Friedrich. Westport, Ct.: Pir Publications, 1991.

Sheikh Muzaffer Ozak al-Jerrahi. *Ashki's Divan*. Translation from the Original Turkish by Muhtar Holland and Sixtina Friedrich. Westport, Ct.: Pir Publications, 1991.

Shaikh ʿAbd al-Qādir al-Jīlānī. *Revelations of the Unseen (Futūḥ al-Ghaib)*. Translated from the Arabic by Muhtar Holland. Houston, Texas: Al-Baz Publishing, Inc., 1992.

Shaikh ʿAbd al-Qādir al-Jīlānī. *The Sublime Revelation (al-Fatḥ ar-Rabbānī)*. Translated from the Arabic by Muhtar Holland. Houston, Texas: Al-Baz Publishing, Inc., 1992.

Shaikh ʿAbd al-Qādir al-Jīlānī. *Utterances (Malfūẓāt)*. Translated from the Arabic by Muhtar Holland. Houston, Texas: Al-Baz Publishing, Inc., 1992.

Shaikh ʿAbd al-Qādir al-Jīlānī. *The Removal of Cares (Jalāʾ al-Khawāṭir)*. Translated from the Arabic by Muhtar Holland. Ft. Lauderdale, Florida: Al-Baz Publishing, Inc., 1997.

Shaikh ʿAbd al-Qādir al-Jīlānī. *Sufficient Provision for Seekers of the Path of Truth (Al-Ghunyali-Ṭālibī Ṭarīq al-Ḥaqq)*. Translated from the Arabic (in 5 vols.) by Muhtar Holland. Hollywood, Florida: Al-Baz Publishing, Inc., 1997.

Shaikh ʿAbd al-Qādir al-Jīlānī. *Fifteen Letters (Khamsatta ʿAshara Maktuban)*. Translated from the Arabic by Muhtar Holland. Hollywood, Florida: Al-Baz Publishing, Inc., 1997.

Shaikh Walī Raslān ad-Dimashqī. *Concerning the Affirmation of Divine Oneness (Risāla fi't-Tawḥīd)*. Translated from the Arabic by Muhtar Holland. Hollywood, Florida: Al-Baz Publishing, Inc., 1997.

Milton Keynes UK
Ingram Content Group UK Ltd.
UKHW020916111124
451035UK00018B/1612

9 789394 770164